Contents

KV-586-669

CHAPTER ONE

Let's Get Started!

CHAPTER ONE
Let's Get Started

So, you're reading a book about periods.

Maybe your mum or dad bought it for you and you're thinking, 'Hmm, it looks like it *could* be interesting – but on the other hand they also recommend **BROCCOLI**.'

Or maybe you found it in the library, or your best friend's bedroom, and were *curious* enough to take a *peek* inside.

OK hang on. You didn't 'borrow' it off your big sister did you?!

WHAAAT?
SHE IS GOING TO KILL YOU!

7

However this book ended up in your hands, I have good news for you. Firstly, it's going to be extremely interesting, and there is literally no broccoli in it at all. Secondly, being curious enough to take a peek into books is a well-known sign of extremely high intelligence – true fact. And thirdly, your sister probably didn't even notice you took it – yet.

Oh, and the other good news – this book is going to change the way you think about periods, forever. It might just

CHANGE YOUR LIFE!

It's going to make you feel excited about getting your period (whether you've already started or are waiting to have one for the first time). It will teach you that even though everybody talks so much about periods, they are just *one part* of a great big beautiful **CYCLE**. Speaking of cycles, this book will help you to become a *Cycle Detective*. By following the clues you get from your body each month, you'll get to know the signs of what's going on in there, understand why you feel the way you do and be able to look after yourself better.

You'll get loads of ideas on how to be your own Body Buddy, S.U.R.F your emotions and *listen* to your body, *trust* your body and *love* your body.

Most of all, you are going to start feeling really, really proud of your period, your amazing body, and all the brilliant things it can do. Aren't you glad you got your hands on this book?

Right then –

Let's Get Started!

★ WAIT A MO! WHAT EVEN IS A PERIOD? ★

Perhaps you're thinking, hang on, I'm not quite sure what a period **IS!** Trust me, this book will give you *a lot* more detail but put *really* simply:

> **A period is the few days each month when a small amount of blood comes out of your vagina.**

Your first period happens during the phase in life you're probably having around now, called *puberty*. But if you don't know too much about this either, don't worry, all of this and more will be explained as we go through this book. Periods are just one part of something called your *menstrual cycle*, which the female body experiences each month (see pages 116–145). For now, rest assured that periods are a part of normal life for most women and girls, just like you, all around the globe.

Cycle Superstars!

Throughout this book I'm going to introduce you to lots of 'Cycle Superstars' – movers, shakers and change-makers – basically people who've seen what needed to be improved about periods and got on and did something about it!

So I thought I'd make the first one – ME!

I'm Milli, a mum of three FANTASTIC children who are all about your age, two girls and a boy. I've also written two other books, both about having babies, and about how, even though women are often a bit scared of giving birth, it can actually be a really positive experience. But all this talking about giving birth got me thinking about another really important part of our lives – PERIODS! I'd noticed that lots of the books and school lessons about periods are pretty outdated and missing out some really important information about things such as cycles and thinking about periods in a more positive way that can be really interesting and extremely helpful!

I found out some of the information in this book by accident, by the time I'd been having my periods for YEARS! I didn't want the same thing to happen to you, so I decided to write a book for girls your age, so that you would have all of this useful knowledge about your body, right from the start. I really hope you enjoy the book and that it makes you feel super positive, proud and excited about the wonders of your body!

PERIODS: FEELING PROUD AND POSITIVE

Periods really are the main event of puberty for most girls, and they are what this book is all about! By the time you've finished reading it, I hope you will be feeling *proud* to be a girl, super *positive* about getting your period and that you have all the information you need.

But at the moment, you might be feeling all sorts of emotions? Perhaps you're excited? Or maybe you are . . .

☑ **NERVOUS?**

☑ **ANXIOUS?**

☑ **EMBARRASSED?**

Or even a bit worried. Maybe you feel a mixture of all those things or something completely different. You might also be unsure about how to talk to your friends or family about periods. It might even make you giggle nervously or feel a little bit awks! It's OK to have these feelings when you're learning about something new, and there's no right or wrong way to feel.

Periods are completely normal, but sometimes people talk about them as if they are something we shouldn't really mention, which doesn't help us feel very positive, does it?! For example, instead of just saying, 'I'm having my period', people use some *really* odd 'code words' and sayings instead, as if periods were something a bit *dreadful* that we should all keep secret. You might hear some quite *boring* code words for periods like:

and a few *odd* ones such as 'a visit from Aunt Flo', 'on the blob' or 'having the painters in'. There are also some quite cute ones like 'in need of medicinal chocolate', 'moon time' or 'wearing the red badge of courage'. Then there are some really terrible ones, such as 'the curse', which, quite frankly, is the kind of negativity nobody needs in their life. But the truth is, whether you choose a cute phrase like 'strawberry week' or tell your friends you are 'stuck at a red traffic light', the effect is the same – you end up covering up what's actually happening!

WHY CAN'T WE JUST SAY, 'PERIOD'?

Well, that's a very interesting question.

The fact is, in lots of different times in history, and in lots of different parts of the world, even today, having your period was thought to be something shameful, embarrassing or even a reason for you to keep away from other people! But periods are not gross, dirty, dangerous or something to be ashamed about. They are just another part of being female, they happen to most of us girls for a big chunk of our lives, and they are normal (and pretty cool!)

We don't have to hide our period, use code words for it, keep it a secret or feel embarrassed about it!

If you are having your period you can do or be anything you like. You can bungee jump, do gymnastics, swim, run, win races and ride rollercoasters. Women on their periods have completed marathons, given speeches in parliament, got promoted in their jobs, looked after their children, made scientific discoveries and created great literature and art. There is literally *nothing* that you can't do when you are having your period.

Yes, you can do ANYTHING!

Cycle Superstars!

CHELLA QUINT

Founder of #PeriodPositive

Period positivity is gaining in popularity more and more, but it was Chella Quint who led the way in saying that periods should not be taboo! Chella was born in Brooklyn, New York and now lives in Sheffield, UK. She was the first person to use the phrase 'period positive' in 2006.

Already working with young people at the time as a teacher, Chella was also an artist who made 'zines' – this is when you design and make your own magazine.

In 2005 she made a zine called *Adventures in Menstruating*, and this made her realise just how much there was to say about periods. She also noticed just how much negativity there is around menstrual products and advertising.

For example, a lot of period adverts suggest it's a good thing if nobody can tell it's a menstrual product from the packaging, or that it's a good thing if nobody can hear us open our tampon wrapper in the toilet. Periods are treated like something we should HIDE!

Chella disagrees.

She designed a charter mark (an award) called the Period Positive Pledge for organisations to earn, and now helps people to think about periods in a new way. She says: 'It's fun to challenge outdated and negative ideas, and talking about it stopped me feeling ashamed. Give it a try!'

Throughout this book, you'll find **Body Buddy Boxes**, filled with ideas and activities for you to try. These boxes will give you lots of ideas of ways to love, nourish and care for your amazing body. Here's the first one, and it's all about tuning in to what your body wants and needs …

Body Buddy Box

Treat Yourself!

What can YOU do for YOURSELF and YOUR BODY today?! Have a think. Tune in. What are you really longing for, needing or craving. Is it a nap? Or would you love to go swimming? Fancy some chocolate? Or maybe you want a big box of strawberries? Perhaps you would like a hug. Or maybe you need a long walk by yourself. Think about something that would make you feel really good today, and take some time to treat yourself and your body to what you really want and need.

CHAPTER TWO

Puberty And Your Brilliant Body

CHAPTER TWO

Puberty And Your Brilliant Body

So we're all agreed that periods are *definitely* nothing to be ashamed of. But have you ever thought about them as something you should *celebrate?!* Well they are! Why? Because your body is literally

AMAZING.

It's brilliant to find out more about how your body works, not only so you can feel prepared for your period and confident that everything is happening as it should, but also so you can *marvel* at the incredible things your body is doing each and every month, without you even having to think about it. As you start to understand your body, you can learn to listen to it, trust it and treat it with the care it deserves. Think of it like developing a friendship – the more you find out about a person, the closer and more connected you feel to them. So let's become even better friends with our bodies, and find out how they work when it comes to all things period, starting with a good look at **PUBERTY**.

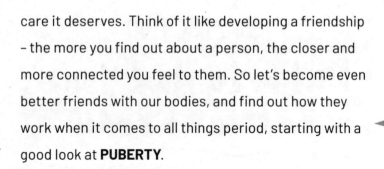

AS IF BY MAGIC: Your body is always changing!

Remember when the Fairy Godmother turns up and with one quick flick of her wand turns Cinderella from a scruffy pumpkin owner into a Princess?! Well, guess what, puberty's *not* like that! It's a *gradual* transformation, and your period definitely doesn't just turn up one day without any warning – abracadabra!

You will probably notice your body slowly changing in a number of ways before you have your period. This is all part of going through puberty, which is basically what happens to all people when their bodies start developing and changing from a child's body to an adult's body. (Glass slippers – optional.)

Puberty changes happen over several years, and start roughly between the ages of eight and 13 for girls and nine to 15 in boys. Puberty is different for everyone though, and everyone's body changes and develops at different speeds and different ages. Because of this, it's not always easy to predict what changes will happen, and when!

All of the changes of puberty are caused by **HORMONES**. You're going to hear that word a lot over the next few years – partly because your grown-ups are going to blame them for everything from your messy bedroom to your sudden ability to eat an entire family size pizza. *'It's her HORMONES.'*

25

But hormones are actually really clever natural chemicals that help control everything from what your body does to how you are feeling. And it's these hormones that will cause some other changes in your body during puberty that you will notice. For girls, these changes, which happen at different ages and speeds for everyone, include:

☑ Getting taller – you will probably 'shoot up' at some point during puberty, and your body will gradually start to look more adult. Your hips usually widen and get bigger.

☑ Breasts beginning to grow – starting with little bumps called 'breast buds', your breasts will gradually develop.

☑ Hair growing in new places – body hair will start to grow on your pubic area and in your armpits.

☑ Sweating more – you might notice that you perspire more and this can cause body odour. You can help prevent this by using underarm deodorant, making sure you bath or shower daily and putting on clean clothes each day.

☑ Greasier hair and skin – hormone changes can cause oily hair and skin, and sometimes this can lead to spots called acne.

Sometimes these might be changes you like, while at other times, they might be changes you feel uncomfortable with or self-conscious about. But whilst puberty is a time when lots of *noticeable* changes can happen quite quickly, here's the big news: *your body is always changing!* From the moment you are born, and throughout your life, you keep changing!

And just like during puberty, you might *like* some of the changes, while some might take a bit more getting used to (ask your Grandad how he felt when his hair fell out!). And have you ever wondered what happens to boys in puberty? Well, they go through lots of changes too, including:

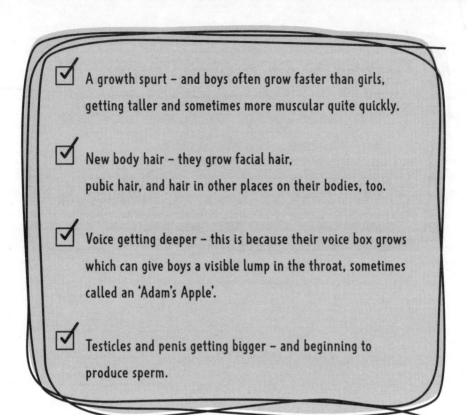

- ☑ A growth spurt – and boys often grow faster than girls, getting taller and sometimes more muscular quite quickly.

- ☑ New body hair – they grow facial hair, pubic hair, and hair in other places on their bodies, too.

- ☑ Voice getting deeper – this is because their voice box grows which can give boys a visible lump in the throat, sometimes called an 'Adam's Apple'.

- ☑ Testicles and penis getting bigger – and beginning to produce sperm.

Just like girls, boys have some temporary effects of puberty too, like greasier skin and hair and acne – and boys can get even more spots than girls! And just like girls, all of these changes can happen at different ages for different boys. Oh, and just like girls, boys can feel excited about some of the changes, but awkward and self-conscious about others. It's different for everyone!

CHANGING BODIES, CHANGING FEELINGS ...

For some young people, puberty is a really difficult time, and the changes in their bodies can feel upsetting. It's OK to feel like this – puberty can be a real rollercoaster, and it can make you think about your body, your identity and who you are, more than you have done before. It's normal to have mixed feelings, to dislike some aspects of your body, or even feel you hate your period. But this almost always gets a lot easier with time, care and support. There is no one size fits all and everyone will have a different journey. If the changes of puberty or how you feel become overwhelming, for whatever reason, talk to a trusted adult, who will be able to guide you towards the support you may need.

UNDERSTANDING YOUR BODY BETTER

As we learn more about puberty and periods, it's really useful to have a look at the parts of your body that are involved, so that we all know exactly what we're talking about. Knowing and using the proper names for stuff is important. Just like periods get called all sorts of strange things, body parts can get the same daft treatment. You might have heard words like 'twinkle', 'foo foo', 'lady bits', 'down there', 'front bottom' and 'minnie' to describe your female body parts. When you think about it, this is a bit odd. We don't call our elbow our 'foldywoldy', do we? So why do we have all these rather odd names for the parts we keep in our pants?!

Worse still, there is a **HUGE** muddle over the proper names **VAGINA** and **VULVA**, with lots of normally intelligent grown-ups calling their *vulva* their *vagina*. Whether people are confused or embarrassed, it's hard to say, but let's put an end to this nonsense immediately and get to know your fabulous femaleness.

WHAT'S BETWEEN MY LEGS?

If you like you can get a mirror, hold it between your legs and see if you can identify all the bits of your own body. Your body won't look exactly like this picture – just like a diagram of a nose might not look exactly like your nose. All bodies are different, and beautiful in different ways.

Female external reproductive organs

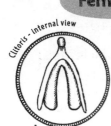

Clitoris - internal view

CLITORIS (RHYMES WITH GLITTER ISS)
The small mound of very sensitive tissue found above the inner labia (see also page 32).

OUTER LABIA
Labia means 'lips' and these are the lip-like folds of skin that edge the vulva. The outer labia grows hairy on the outside during puberty.

VULVA
This is the correct word for the whole external area of the female sexual organs and includes the labia and clitoris.

URETHRA
This is the very tiny hole where your pee comes out. That's all it's for. Pee.

VAGINA
The passage where the blood comes out during your period. Babies also come out of the vagina when they are born. Actually, you can only see the opening to your vagina in this diagram (the vaginal vestibule). The rest is inside of you (see page 37).

HYMEN
A thin circle or semi-circle of skin at the entrance to your vagina, usually with a hole or holes in the middle.

INNER LABIA
These are the thinner 'lips' that surround the entrance to the vagina and the urethra.

PERINEUM
The skin between your vagina and anus.

ANUS
This is the hole where your poo comes out.

MORE ABOUT THE CLITORIS

What you can see of the clitoris is only the 'head' inside a little fold of skin known as the 'hood'. The whole clitoris is actually much larger, between 7 and 12 cm long in adults, and extends inside you. The clitoris, along with the vagina and vulva, are very sensitive, and stimulation of these areas through sex (see pages 40–41) or masturbation, can lead to an intense pleasurable feeling called an orgasm.

What is masturbation? Masturbation is the word for when you touch or rub your own clitoris, vagina and vulva, or, if you are a boy, your penis, in private. Not everyone does this, but it's totally normal to explore your body in this way.

AM I NORMAL?

As with all parts of our bodies, sometimes people wonder if their vulva looks 'normal'. Some girls and women worry about it because we don't usually get to see many other vulvas, and we can sometimes make the mistake of thinking that ours is different or even 'strange'. But in fact, vulvas come in a huge variety of shapes and forms.

And they are all PERFECTLY normal.

As you go through puberty, you might notice other differences too. Breasts and nipples, for example, can come in all different shapes, sizes and colours! Body hair, too, can be straight, curly, thick, thin, dark or lighter, and sometimes grow in places you weren't expecting, like on your belly, top lip or even on your breasts! The truth is, we are all beautifully different.

As you grow up, experimenting with how you look by using make-up, hair dye and body hair removal can be fun, but don't forget to love yourself as you are, too. This is sometimes called being 'Body Positive'. Being body positive means getting to know your body, understanding it and treating it with love and kindness, like a friend.

★ YOUR BODY BELONGS TO YOU! ★

Sometimes people call your vulva and vagina – and all the other bits between your legs – your 'private parts'. This is because they belong to you, and they are private. You never have to show them to anyone, let anyone touch them or see them, even in a photo or on a screen, unless you want to, because they are YOURS. Sometimes a doctor or a member of your family might need to see your private parts, but they should ALWAYS explain why and ask your permission first. Even if it's a doctor or someone you trust and know well, if something doesn't feel right, or you feel uncomfortable, talk to another grown-up who you trust.

Remember: No means no. If you don't want someone to touch you anywhere on your body, not just on your private parts, they should respect your body boundaries. This means any kind of touch, even what some people see as 'fun' touch, such as tickling or play fighting, should not happen without your agreement – known as your 'consent'. Consent is when you agree to something because you really want it to happen, not because someone is pressuring you or you feel you have to. If something doesn't feel right to you, you can say stop. If you say **stop**, this should always mean **stop**.

ITS ALWAYS YOUR BODY AND YOUR CHOICE.

If you are worried about any of this and want to speak to someone who can definitely help, you can call Childline on 0800 1111 or visit https://www.childline.org.uk/.

Body Buddy Box

Take Up Space

Sometimes, if we change what our body is doing on the outside, it can change how we feel on the inside. This exercise is designed to help you feel more confident and brave.

Stand with both your feet on the ground, the same distance apart as your hips. Roll your shoulders around in circles and let them relax. Take a few deep breaths in and out. Raise your arms above your head, then bend forwards from your waist, flopping towards the floor. Let yourself hang there for a moment, with your arms dangling. Then slowly begin to uncurl yourself, coming up straighter and straighter, until you are standing tall again with your arms by your sides. Now imagine there is a string between the top of your head and the ceiling, gently pulling you up taller. Keep your your feet flat on the floor, but stretch yourself up towards the sky. Take a deep breath and let it slowly out. Feel how tall you are, and notice how this makes you feel on the inside. Say aloud, **'I AM IMPORTANT'**. Try doing this exercise often, and, as you go about your day at home or at school, remember to make sure you are walking tall, and taking up all the space you need.

WHAT'S INSIDE A FEMALE BODY?

Now let's have a look *inside* the female body, which is also very interesting. These are the parts that you *can't* see and might never have really thought about, but they do some really amazing and clever things.

Interesting fact! Your uterus is held in place by a kind of 'hammock' of muscles, called your pelvic floor muscles. It's useful to know about these muscles because, as you get older, and especially after having a baby, they can get weaker. The most common thing to happen if your pelvic floor muscles are weak is that you might leak wee when you cough or sneeze. But just like some of the other muscles in your body, you can actually exercise your pelvic floor and help to keep it strong! You don't need to do this until later in life, but if you want to feel where they are before then, just squeeze as if you are trying to stop doing a wee, and you will feel them working. Clever stuff!

Female internal reproductive organs

FALLOPIAN TUBES
After an egg is released, it travels from your ovary along one of the fallopian tubes and to your uterus.

OVARIES
You have one ovary on each side and they are where eggs are stored and released during a time known as ovulation.

EGGS
These are the female sex cells and if fertilised by male sex cells (sperm), they can make a baby. Eggs are the largest human cell and are the only cell visible to the naked eye.

CERVIX
The cervix is the entrance to your uterus from the vagina.

UTERUS
Also known as your womb (rhymes with room), this is the organ or 'room' where a baby grows. It's usually the same size and shape as an upside-down pear.

VAGINA
The strong and stretchy tube that leads from your vulva to your uterus.

SO WHAT EXACTLY IS A PERIOD?

OK. So now we have learned more about our beautiful bodies, inside and out, we can start to understand in *more* detail what actually happens when you have a period. We have already talked about how your period is:

The few days each month when a small amount of blood comes out of your vagina.

BUT WHAT DOES THIS MEAN AND WHY DOES IT HAPPEN?

Each month the female body goes through a process, called a 'menstrual cycle'.

COMPETING EGGS: Your ovaries contain little sacs called follicles where there are always eggs in different stages of development. Each month, some of these eggs start to get bigger and stronger, ready to be released. It's almost like a competition to see which egg will be the chosen one!

THE WINNING EGG: The 'winning egg' (usually the biggest and strongest) is then released from one of your ovaries and travels down the nearby fallopian tube. (If you are a non-identical twin, congratulations, this means TWO eggs were released to make you and your sibling!)

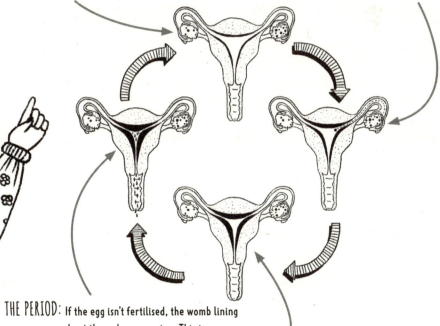

THE PERIOD: If the egg isn't fertilised, the womb lining comes away and out through your vagina. This is your period. Only about half of your period is 'blood' – the rest is mostly the lining of your uterus, along with vaginal fluids, which are a mucous or gel-like substance made by the cells of the cervix (more about these fluids on pages 155-158). It's often a reddish-brown colour, a bit darker than the bright red blood you see when you cut yourself (although it can be bright red too).

SLEEPOVER READY: At the same time the lining of your uterus thickens and gets soft and cushiony, waiting for the egg to arrive – a bit like making your bedroom all nice for your friend to come on a sleepover. If the egg is fertilised by sperm, this is where a baby will grow.

WHY DO WE HAVE PERIODS?

Your period is part of your body maturing so that your body is prepared to get pregnant, if this is ever something you decide you want to do. **But don't panic!** Getting pregnant is something that can only happen to you if you have sex.

You might find it awkward talking about sex, but it is important to know how babies are made.

Sex (or sexual intercourse) is something that grown-up people do together, most often for closeness, pleasure and fun. Sex can happen between two people of the same sex, or different sexes, but to make a baby, the two people having sex need to be biologically male and female. They usually kiss, cuddle and get sexually excited. For the man, this means his penis gets hard, or erect, and for the woman, this means her vagina and vulva get slippery and wet. Sometimes, but not always, the penis goes inside the vagina, and this is called vaginal sex.

During sex both men and women may experience an orgasm. This is when they reach the peak of their excitement. When a man has an orgasm, he releases a fluid called semen that contains millions of tiny cells called sperm.

If the man and woman are having vaginal sex, the sperm are released into the woman's body and they try to reach her egg. If one of the male sperm joins up with the female egg, it is called fertilisation. The fertilised egg then travels down into the soft, comfy uterus lining. It will attach to this lining and develop slowly into a baby – this takes around 40 weeks. The woman's periods will stop when this happens until some time after the baby is born. This is one of the first signs a woman has that she may be pregnant – her period does not come when she expects it to. If grown-ups want to have vaginal sex just for pleasure, and not to get pregnant, they can use something called contraception, which works in different ways to stop the sperm getting to the egg.

Sometimes grown-ups who want to have a baby together find that, even though they have sex without contraception, the woman does not get pregnant. If this happens, they can try other ways of making a baby, for example a method called IVF, where an egg is taken and fertilised with sperm in a laboratory, and then put back into a woman's body to grow. This is sometimes called being a 'test tube baby', and if this is how you were made, it makes you very special!

When you first learn about sex it can sound a bit strange, but it's not something to worry about. Sex is something that should only happen when you feel completely ready and are with another person that you trust and respect, and who trusts and respects you too. It should never happen unless you 'consent', which means that you say clearly that you really want it to happen and don't have any doubts about it. In the UK, the age at which you are considered ready and able to give your consent is 16, but many people don't have sex until they are older than that.

★ DO PETS HAVE PERIODS?! ★

If you've got a female pet dog you might have noticed them getting a bit of what looks like blood coming from their vagina once in a while ... but is this a period? Technically, NOPE.

Most mammals – including dogs – have a different kind of cycle to us, called an ESTROUS cycle. This is sometimes called being 'in season' or 'in heat' and it happens when they are the MOST ready to become pregnant. Lots of mammals with estrous cycles, especially larger animals, only have one or two 'seasons' per year, and not all of them have 'blood'. The blood-like liquid you see when dogs (and foxes and wolves) are 'in season' is not the lining of the uterus, as it is with human periods. It's simply a liquid caused by hormonal changes.

Very few creatures on earth have a menstrual cycle like we do, mainly some (but not all) primates such as gorillas, chimps and monkeys and also BATS, the ELEPHANT SHREW and the SPINY MOUSE. And that's it!

See, told you,

YOU ARE SPECIAL!

CHAPTER THREE

All About Period Products

CHAPTER THREE
All About
Period Products

When you have your period, you will need to choose what product you want to use to catch or absorb your period blood. You might notice that sometimes period products are called things like 'Sanitary Towels' and 'Feminine Hygiene', but it's probably time we stopped using old fashioned words like these, because they make it sound like periods are not very clean or hygienic. In this book, just like we call periods, 'periods', we are going to call period products, 'period products'!

So now let's learn a little bit more about the different products you can choose from – and as you are about to discover, there are quite a lot of different options! As we go through them, you can start thinking about what might be right for you.

CHOOSING YOUR PERIOD PRODUCTS

Lots of things will influence what period products you use, including family, money, comfort, exercise and how light or heavy your period is. But what's important is that you're happy and comfortable with what you decide to use. You might also find that you end up using different products for different days or occasions – tampons or menstrual cups for swimming, period pants for running or pads for night time – it will take a while and a bit of experimenting to find your faves. And your faves might change! You will probably have your period for quite a lot of your life – and you might find that you get to like some products more than others, or even that new and fantastic products are invented over time. It can be fun to experiment!

TRY THIS! Have a Period Product Party! Get a group of your friends to come round and each bring a different product. Open them all up and explore! If you're not sure about a party, maybe just you and your BFF could get a few products out of the packaging and see what they are like.

Here's some info about some of the main products that are currently available:

✦ DISPOSABLE PADS

Another word for these is 'sanitary towels' but since we have no time for anything that suggests your period is dirty, I'm not going to call them that! I think a better name is just 'pads', because that's what they are – pads … for your period! Disposable pads are usually made of fibres with an absorbent layer hidden inside. They have a sticky strip on the bottom – you peel off the cover of this strip and stick this bit to your knickers, like this:

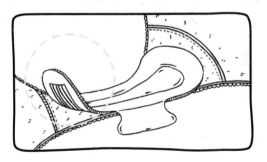

You can buy different types of pads depending on how heavy or light your period is (see pages 89-90), and special extra big ones for using overnight. Whichever you choose, in the daytime you will need to change your

pad every 3 or 4 hours, or more often if your flow is heavier. When you have taken it off, *never* flush it down the loo (this can cause a blockage or end up in seas and rivers – yikes!), but instead roll it up and then wrap it in either toilet paper or the wrapper that it came in (or the wrapper of the next pad). In public toilets there is a special bin beside the loo for period products, and at home you can just throw it into your bathroom bin.

✦ WINGS OR NO WINGS?

I'm sorry to be the bearer of some seriously disappointing news, but unfortunately the kind of wings you get on period pads are *not* the kind you can fly with. In fact, they are not particularly exciting in any way, shape or form, sadly. Pads with wings just have a little extra bit on each side like this:

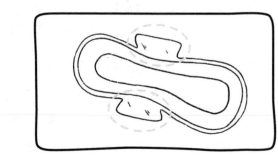

The wings also have a sticky strip that you tuck round and attach to the *outside* of your knickers, to help keep the pad in place.

You can get disposable pads with wings and without wings. Some people like the ones with wings because they are less likely to slide around and can be better for preventing leaks (see pages 186-188), other people like the ones without wings because they are easier to attach. Like all period products, the only way to work out which you prefer is to try them both.

✦ REUSABLE PADS

Many disposable pads contain a **LOT** of plastic and chemicals and can take over

FIVE HUNDRED YEARS

to biodegrade, break down and rot away (see pages 68-69). For this reason, some people like to use washable cloth pads, which you use, wash and reuse. Reusable cloth pads come in lots of cool and fun designs and

just like disposable pads, they also come in different sizes and soak up different amounts of period blood for different stages of your period.

All reusable pads have wings with poppers – this is how you attach them to your underwear. You usually wear them with the design side 'up' (yes you bleed onto that lovely pattern that you spent ages choosing!), and then you just click together the poppers underneath your underwear.

You will need several reusable pads if you are thinking about using them for every period, but you could start with two or three and see how you like them. How many you will need, if you decide to only use reusable pads, depends on your flow, and how often the laundry happens in your house. A good guide would be how many disposable pads you use in each period, because you need to change reusable pads roughly as often as you would change a disposable.

52

When you change your reusable pad, you can use the poppers to fold them up with the blood on the inside, like this:

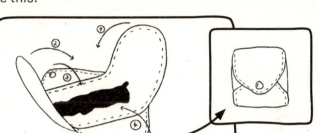

It's great if you can get them soaking in water as soon as possible, but if you are at school or out and about, it's a good idea to have a small cloth bag with you and pop any worn reusable pads in there until you get home.

Reusable pads cost quite a lot when you get started – around £80 to £100 if you want around 20 pads – but should last about five years, so in the long run, they work out cheaper than disposable pads, which cost roughly the same amount for just one year. And if you are crafty, you could even sew your own! They are a little tricky, and you will probably need a grown-up to help you, but you can find instructions online.

TIP

When you soak your pads add a couple of drops of your favourite essential oil to the water then pop them in the wash. Lemon is LOVELY!

✦ PERIOD PANTS

These are another fairly new invention and at first, they don't seem to make sense! A pair of pants? (Let's just be clear, I don't mean period TROUSERS here, these are special KNICKERS!) What, nothing else? Just ... **PANTS?!** But yes, they really are just a special pair of pants that look pretty normal from the outside, but with an extra absorbent layer 'built in' so that you can wear them **ALL DAY!** They absorb about the same amount of period blood as around four tampons, so you can just pull them on and get on with your day. There are special designs from a few companies for teens and pre-teens, and while, like reusable pads, they are expensive at around £20 a pair, they should last you for several years if you look after them. You can also use them alongside other period products. For example, you could wear them as an extra precaution if you are worried about your tampon leaking if your flow is particularly heavy. Or you could wear them around the time your period is due – just-in-case.

NEWS FLASH! You can now get period **SWIMWEAR** that works the same way as the **PANTS**! So you can keep swimming during your period, even if you don't use tampons or cups.

MENSTRUAL CUPS

Often called mooncups (Mooncup was the brand name of the very first silicone cup when it launched in 2002), this type of period wear can take a bit of practice, and they're probably not right for your first period – although it's always up to you! Menstrual cups are made of silicone (soft, rubbery stuff) and shaped like a small cone.

IMPORTANT NOTE! WASH YOUR HANDS BEFORE INSERTING A CUP AND BEFORE REMOVAL.

1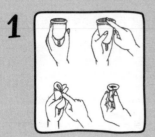

First, fold the cup to make it easier to insert. Push one side of the rim down into the cup, creating a narrow point.

2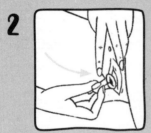

Either standing with one leg on a loo seat, or seated (whichever you find easiest), hold your labia apart and slowly insert the folded cup into your vagina, aiming up towards the tailbone. When you are no longer able to keep it folded, let it open inside you. Continue to push it gently inside until the stem is no longer visible.

3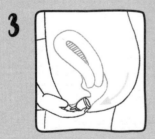

To remove the cup, sit on the loo and pull gently on the stem of the cup, until you are able to reach the base. Pinching the base of the cup will break the vacuum seal and make it much easier to remove.

The cup 'catches' your period blood, and you need to remove it and empty it into the toilet around every four hours, and up to a maximum of 12 hours, depending on your flow. You then simply rinse it and reinsert. Then, when your period finishes, sterilise your cup by boiling it in water for about seven minutes. You only need to buy one menstrual cup (they cost about £20) and it should last years and years – making them a great choice for both your wallet and the environment. Getting cups in – and out – can take a bit of practice! Some people say it takes about three periods before you get the hang of a cup. If your mum, big sister or another woman in your life uses a cup, then they might be able to help you, or you can find informative and and detailed instructions on the website for your brand of cup. You can get menstrual cups especially made for teenagers (basically they are a bit smaller).

TIP

You don't need to rinse your cup every time you empty it. You can just wipe it clean with toilet paper. However, if you want to rinse it and are wearing your cup anywhere you use public toilets, you can carry a bottle of water into the loo with you, to save you having to rinse it in a public sink (which might make you feel . . . AWKS!). Just pour the water from the bottle and rinse your cup over the toilet, then wipe dry with loo paper.

✴ MENSTRUAL DISCS

Very similar to cups, made of
silicon, cost about £20, but
shaped like a disc!

The cups sit inside your body just below your cervix
(see page 37) and extend down into your vagina,
whereas discs just sit right up there near your cervix.

IMPORTANT NOTE! WASH YOUR HANDS BEFORE INSERTING
A MENSTRUAL DISC AND BEFORE REMOVAL.

 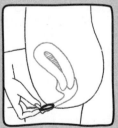 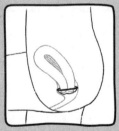

To insert the disc, first, squeeze the rim so that it forms an '8' shape. This makes it
easier to insert. Once you have placed it as far as your fingers will allow, release the
grip you have on it, and it should spring into place!

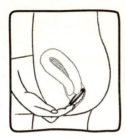 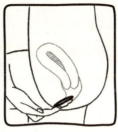

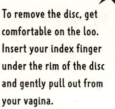
To remove the disc, get comfortable on the loo. Insert your index finger under the rim of the disc and gently pull out from your vagina.

Just like cups, discs take a bit of practice, and you probably need to try them alongside other products at first. But once you have the knack, you might never look back – **AND**, just like cups, they are brilliant for the environment too.

TAMPONS

Tampons are usually made of a mix of cotton and human-made fibres. Tampons with applicators look like this:

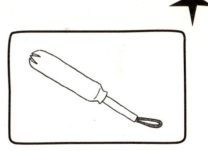

Some tampons come without applicators, and you insert them with your fingers. They look like this:

You insert them into your vagina, where they sit inside you and absorb your period blood. It's usually easier to insert and remove them when your period is heavier.

IMPORTANT NOTE! WASH YOUR HANDS BEFORE INSERTING A TAMPON AND BEFORE REMOVAL.

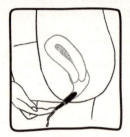 

Either standing with one leg on a loo seat or seated on the loo if it is more comfortable for you, insert the tip of the applicator into your vaginal opening. Slide it slowly into your vagina until your fingers holding the grip are touching your vulva. Then push the plunger of the applicator all the way in – this releases the tampon into the correct position. Remove the applicator and discard it.

Tampons don't go very far inside you, but you shouldn't be able to feel them **once they are inserted**. They have a string attached to them that hangs outside of your vagina. This string shouldn't poke out from your knickers or swimming costume, but if you are worried, you can tuck it gently just inside your labia.

To remove your tampon, you just pull gently on the string.

Just like disposable pads, disposable tampons should **NOT** be flushed down the toilet – they can cause blockages in drains and sewers or worse still end up polluting the sea!

Tampons are normally safe, but they can cause a serious medical condition called Toxic Shock Syndrome (TSS). This is very rare, but it's important to know about it if you are going to use tampons. There is always information on tampon packaging about TSS. Always read this packaging and remember to change your tampon regularly, around every four hours.

✳ REUSABLE TAMPONS

Just like you can get reusable cloth pads, you can also get tampons that work in the same way. So if you decide that tampons are for you, but are worried about the environment or the chemicals and plastic that many of them contain, you could consider reusable tampons. They are made of 100% organic cotton and you roll them up and tie a string to secure the tampon, before inserting just like you would a disposable one. They stay in the same length of time – around four to six hours, and then you wash them in the washing machine and reuse them.

★ MENSTRUAL SPONGES

Another environmentally friendly choice, these are **LITERALLY** sea sponges which you insert like a tampon, then remove, wash and reuse! The advantages are that sea sponge is sustainable – it's like a crop that grows back after a harvest. Some people find that menstrual sponges are very comfortable and cheap compared to buying pads or tampons each month – each one costs around £10 and should last six months to a year. However, some girls and women find them hard to remove, messy and impractical for use outside the home. They're definitely worth a try though if you want to explore your eco-options!

Cycle Superstars!

LAURA CORYTON
Founder of Stop Taxing Periods

In May 2014 Laura Coryton was a 22-year-old university student in London when she decided to start a petition to ask the UK government to stop the 'Tampon Tax'. Tax is an extra charge on things you buy that goes to the government, and Laura thought it was unfair that people had to pay tax on period products, because for women and girls, these are essential items!

She was helped by Dawn Primarolo, who in 2000 had campaigned in her job as a Member of Parliament (MP) to have the tax on menstrual products reduced. Laura thought this was brilliant, but wanted the government to do even more and get rid of it completely.

Laura's petition got over 300,000 signatures, and she was even supported by Barack Obama, who, at the time, was the President of the United States! With the help of another MP called Paula Sheriff, they proudly 'got the world talking about periods'. The Tampon Tax was abolished in the UK on 1 January 2021, but there are still lots of other countries in the world, for example Hungary, Sweden, Mexico, Spain, China and several US states, where the tax still exists. Perhaps you could campaign about this or another issue you are passionate about. As Laura says, 'It's important to never give up on something you believe in, especially when it unfairly targets over half of our population simply because they're women.'

★ FREE PERIOD PRODUCTS ★

If your family can't afford period products, you are not alone. Around 1 in 10 girls in the UK have been unable to buy pads or tampons, and this number can be the same or even higher in other parts of the world. This is a global problem, and is sometimes known as 'period poverty'. Not being able to access the period products you need can really hold you back from getting on with your life, preventing you from going to school, playing sport or even making it hard for you to leave the house.

If affording period products is a problem for your family, you can save money by buying supermarket value brands of pads and tampons, which usually work just as well as the more expensive brands, or you could consider switching to reusable period products like cloth pads or a cup, which also work out cheaper. In the UK, you should now be able to get free period products from your school, and you can also get free period products from some food banks.

If your family are lucky enough not to have to worry about affording menstrual products, you could donate extra packets of tampons and pads to your local food bank, and also make sure your school are offering plenty of free supplies, so that other young people are able to get the products they need.

Cycle Superstars!

AMIKA GEORGE

Founder of #FreePeriods

Amika George was born in 1999 and lives in North London. When she was 18 she started a petition, asking the UK Prime Minister at the time, Theresa May, to give free period products to all girls in the UK who were eligible for free school meals. Amika was worried to hear that girls were missing school because they couldn't afford period products and felt that this should change.

She didn't think that many people would be interested in her petition, but in just a few weeks, around 2,000 people signed it, and within a year, around 200,000 had added their names!

That same year, Amika organised a march in London where over 2,000 people protested about period poverty. This action, along with her petition and action from other groups such as the Red Box Project and Bloody Good Period, made the government take action. And, in 2019, it was announced that period products would be free in all UK schools.

Amika was rightly very proud of what she had achieved. When she was asked what she hopes will be next to change she said, 'I'd like to think that the idea of embarrassment and shame about periods will be gone. People are starting to question this idea that menstruation is disgusting.'

★ GO GREEN FOR RED ★

Helping the environment when you have your period

The invention of disposable pads and tampons might have felt genius at the time, but these days the world is waking up to waste – and period waste is a seriously big problem.

✶ The average woman will use around 11,000 tampons and pads over her lifetime.

✶ Disposable pads are around 90 per cent plastic. One pack of pads is equal to FOUR plastic bags – and we all know how we feel about plastic bags!

✶ Tampons can also contain plastic! Even non-applicator tampons can contain as much as 6 per cent plastic. Plus wrappers and applicators are usually plastic.

✶ In the UK, pads and tampons amount to 200,000 tonnes of landfill EVERY YEAR.

✶ More than 45 billion tampons and pads are used every year across the globe resulting in 3.2 million kilograms of waste.

✶ The Marine Conservation Society reports that 4.8 menstrual products are found for every 100 metres of beach cleaned. Most of these get there by being flushed down the toilet.

★ Tampons and pads take around 500 YEARS to break down and 'biodegrade'. This means that if they had been used by the six wives of Henry VIII, they would only just be disappearing now!

★ As they biodegrade, they create tiny pieces of plastic, known as MICROPLASTICS, which pollute our rivers and oceans and cause damage to life on earth.

Heard enough?! So what can you do about this? Well, the best thing you can do is to switch away from using plastic in as many areas of your life as possible. If you want to go plastic free for your periods, but you still want to use disposable pads or tampons, you could try to buy period products that are plastic free. Look for words on the packaging like 'plastic free', 'biodegradable' or 'compostable'. If you can't find these, the disposable period products with the least plastic are non-applicator tampons.

OR

Switch to reusables. Try period pants, reusable pads and menstrual cups. See pages 51-59 for more about these period products, which can also be a cheaper option.

Cycle Superstars!

ELLA DAISH

Campaigner to #EndPeriodPlastic

Ella Daish was doing her job delivering the post in 2018 when she noticed the amount of rubbish she was seeing on her route was getting worse and worse. She felt like taking action and decided to make some changes in her own life, switching to reusable water bottles and make-up wipes instead of disposable ones. However, about a week later, when she was having her own period, a thought suddenly hit her: how much plastic waste each woman creates with *every single menstrual cycle*.

Ella decided to do something. She launched a campaign to #EndPeriodPlastic, calling on big supermarkets and manufacturers to remove *all* plastic from their period products. Her petition has nearly 250,000 signatures and so far she has persuaded several large supermarket chains in the UK to stop the production of their own-brand plastic tampon applicators, which collectively saves over 17 tonnes of plastic annually! Lil-Lets, Superdrug and Morrisons have reacted to the campaign by launching and developing their own eco-friendly ranges, giving their customers the chance to avoid buying products containing plastic. Ella hopes other companies will soon follow.

I asked Ella for her advice to young people who want to get involved in her campaign. 'It's so important that you know you can make a difference,' she told me. 'I never thought I could do anything like this, but look what I've achieved! So raise your voices! Start conversations with your friends about the plastic in tampons and pads. This flow of discussion creates a wave of awareness, action and change. It is powerful!'

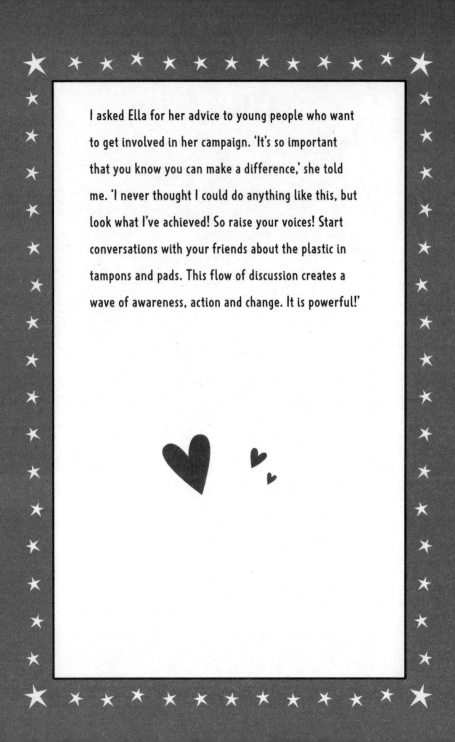

Move Your Body!

We all spend a lot of time on screens these days but don't forget to make time for fun activities that involve moving and stretching your fabulous body. You don't have to be sporty to enjoy moving, it's just about finding something that you like. How about:

✦ Going for a walk (take a dog if you can!)

✦ Swimming

✦ Playing outside with friends, e.g. tag, catch or just running and racing about

✦ Playing in the sea if you live near it (with an adult to keep you safe)

✦ Dancing (at a class or in your bedroom!)

✦ Yoga (lots of videos online to try)

✦ Skateboarding

✦ Going on a bike or scooter

✦ Trying a new team sport such as netball or football

✦ Gardening

Nothing is impossible, not even when you're on your period!

CHAPTER FOUR

My First Period

CHAPTER FOUR
My First Period

MENARCHE MALARKY: GETTING TO GRIPS WITH THE BASICS

We usually know the dates for our school terms, what days we have our favourite lessons and when it's going to be our next birthday. But there is one event that we can't predict in the same way – our very first period. Some people call this 'starting' and the proper word for it is 'menarche' (which, confusingly, is pronounced men-ar-key – why can't things just be written how they are spelt?!).

The age at which your first period happens varies quite a lot from person to person. Some girls have their menarche at eight, whilst others might be 16. The average age to start is 12 or 13.

And the actual day that you start is top secret – literally *nobody* knows when it will be exactly – not even you!

This might feel quite fun and exciting, but it can also feel a little bit daunting. You might have a lot of questions about what it will be like, how you know it's happening and what to do. Let's go through a few of them and help you go from concerned to confident! Learning and understanding can help you feel so much stronger, in fact, some people even say

KNOWLEDGE IS POWER!

WHAT ARE THE SIGNS I MIGHT GET MY PERIOD SOON?

Although knowing exactly when your period will start is impossible, this is the time to start thinking like a Cycle Detective. There's more about this on pages 125–128, but put simply, being a Cycle Detective is about listening to your body and following the clues. And if you do this, you might get a better idea of whether your first period will turn up soon ... or take a little while longer! But whether you start your period earlier than your friends, at the same time or you are the last of your group – don't worry: each person is different and there is no 'right' or 'wrong' time.

There are two main places to look for clues:

★ CLUE 1: Family history

Speak to any female members of your family, such as your mum, sisters, grandma or aunts – can you find out when they started their period? It's possible your body will follow a similar pattern, but it's not guaranteed.

✦ CLUE 2: Changes to your body

As we've already covered, puberty is different for everyone, but it does *usually* follow similar patterns. Here's the chain of body-changing events to look out for:

NIPPLE AND BREAST CHANGES

This is usually the first change you will notice. Your period is probably two to three years away.

☑️ A firm, round lump forms beneath each nipple. This can happen on one side before the other. These are called 'breast buds' and can be a bit sore when you touch them.

☑️ The circle around each nipple, called the 'areola', gets bigger and darker.

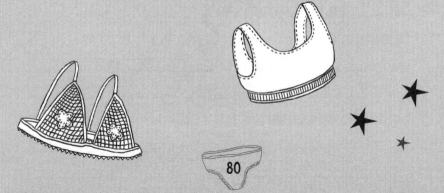

80

★ EXTRA CLUES, FROM YOUR BOOBS! ★

Did you know ... the changes in your breasts can give you an idea of how close your first period is, depending on how old you are when they happen. Amazing, right?! So if you are *younger* when your breasts start changing, say around eight, this usually means it could be up to three years before your period starts. But if you are a bit *older*, say 13 before your boobs change, it will usually take less time for you to start your period and you could get it within a year. And if your breasts start growing somewhere in the *middle* of all that, at around ten or 11, you'll probably get your period in about two years. It's not an exact science, but these are definitely good clues!

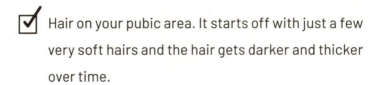

PUBIC HAIR

This is usually the second change you notice.

☑ Hair on your pubic area. It starts off with just a few very soft hairs and the hair gets darker and thicker over time.

☑ Around the same time as your first pubic hairs (sometimes called 'pubes') appear, you might notice the skin on your face getting oilier and spotty, your hair getting greasier or body odour.

BODY SHAPE

This is usually the final change you notice.

☑ As well as your breasts growing, your hips might widen. You might need bigger underwear and trousers than you did a little while ago.

☑ You might notice that you grow taller in quite a short space of time. If you have a very big and fast growth spurt, this could mean your period is about six months to a year away.

☑ You might see other changes in your body as it possibly grows curvier, softer, wider and taller.

☑ Your vulva will change too. If you are looking at this part of your body in the mirror (see page 31), you might notice the labia or lips growing and changing, and your clitoris getting slightly bigger.

VAGINAL FLUID

As you will find out lots more about on pages 148–158, your vagina will be drier or more moist, depending on where you are in your menstrual cycle. On the most moist days, the types of fluid – sometimes called 'discharge' – can be quite different. It can vary from a thin and watery liquid to a thick and sticky substance. You might notice your vagina being more moist around six months to a year before your first period, and then, as you get closer to your first period, you might notice different types of fluid in your underwear, as your menstrual cycle gets underway.

SO, IS THERE REALLY NO WAY OF KNOWING THE ACTUAL DAY WHEN MY FIRST PERIOD WILL COME?!

No, there isn't. Sorry! Although, if you *listen to your body*, you *might* notice other, subtler clues – both for when your first period might arrive and for the next ones after that. For example, you might feel changes in your energy levels. You might also notice changes in your moods, such as feeling more tearful, angry or extra happy. You might get spots on your face, tender boobs or see changes in your vaginal fluid. You might feel bloated or have uncomfortable, crampy feelings in your lower tummy where your uterus is. Some women say that they even have what is called an 'intuitive' feeling that something is about to happen. This is when you just 'know' something, but can't really explain *how* you know.

It's a DEEP kind of knowing.

But even if you have signs from your body, or from a deep kind of feeling, the exact timing of it will probably still surprise you. One day you will just look in your knickers or on your sheets and see period blood. But this 'not knowing' isn't something to worry about because after finishing this book, you will know exactly what to do when the time comes.

WHAT CAN I DO TO GET READY?

Being prepared can help you to feel less worried about things. This is true about all kinds of things in life, and periods are no different! Reading this book is one really good way of getting prepared. And putting together your first period kit (see pages 104-107) and always having it in your school bag, will help too. Apart from that, you don't need to *do* anything! Just enjoy the excitement of waiting for this new phase of your life to begin!

HOW WILL I KNOW IT HAS STARTED?

You might feel damp between your legs and if, for example, you are at school and feel like your period might be starting in class, you can just ask your teacher if you can be excused, and go and have a quick check in the toilets. You might notice your period has started when you use the toilet and see blood on the paper after you have wiped. Or your period might start in the night and you might wake up to find blood on your PJs or sheets.

Some first periods are 'light' (see pages 89-90) and often, girls are not sure at first if 'this is it', or not! If you are in doubt, put a pad in your underwear anyway and carry on with your day. If nothing else happens, it could have been a little bit of ovulation spotting (see page 134), or maybe just a little bit of poo that got mixed with your discharge when you wiped or because you didn't quite wipe properly earlier in the day. Some girls do have 'heavy' first periods, which has the advantage of making it much easier to know that you've started, but can be a bit overwhelming. Remember, everyone's periods are different and there's no right or wrong way to experience your first period. If you are worried or need help, talk to a friend or a grown-up you trust.

WHAT WILL IT LOOK LIKE?

You might be expecting period blood to be ketchup red, like the kind of blood you see if you cut yourself. But your period doesn't always look like this, even once you are a bit older and your menstrual cycles have become more settled. First period blood – and all period blood –

can look dark red, brownish, rusty coloured or pinkish rather than bright red, especially on the first day. And it can also be ketchup red! Everyone's different, but you will gradually learn what's normal for you as you get to know your periods and menstrual cycle better.

WHAT DO I DO WHEN IT ACTUALLY STARTS?

If you think your period has started, you might feel like you want to clean yourself up with some toilet paper, tissues or wipes. Change your underwear if you need to, and reach for your chosen period product.

WHAT SHOULD I USE FOR MY FIRST PERIOD?

There are no 'right' or 'wrong' period products to use for your first period, and you can read all about the different options in Chapter 3. Many girls use a pad for their first-ever period, and then, as they get to know more about their period, they experiment with other products.

Some girls find that internal products such as menstrual cups and tampons are not comfortable for their first periods, especially if their periods are lighter. This is because, if your vagina is drier, they can be difficult to insert and remove. Some people also like to stick to products such as pads and menstrual cups because they can see their period, and this helps them notice any changes in how heavy their period is. It's also great to talk to your friends and grown-ups to decide which product you feel most confident with.

Pssst ... some period products, such as tampons, need changing about every four hours, so make sure you check the instructions carefully before you use them. During your first few periods, you might like to check more often to see if they need changing sooner. After a few months, you will get to know your period better and feel more confident.

WHAT IS 'FLOW'?

You might have seen or heard the expressions 'light flow', 'medium flow' and 'heavy flow' used to describe periods. 'Flow' basically means how much period blood there is during your period, and it varies for different people on different days.

Most people have a heavier flow at the start of their period – which means there'll be a bit more period blood – and it gets lighter towards the end – which means there'll be less period blood. This might mean that on the first day or two you need to choose products for 'heavy flow' and also change them more often. Your flow can also be heavy at night – if so make sure you choose period products for night-time AND heavy flow, and put an old towel over your sheets for extra reassurance.

You might notice that your flow is lighter at night, because you are lying down, but that when you stand up in the morning, gravity means you suddenly have a heavier flow – which can take you by surprise! Some people have very heavy periods, especially during their teenage years while their cycles are getting settled. Other people have light periods, where they don't bleed that much. If your period is very heavy, or if the flow you have got used to changes in any way, make sure you are looking after yourself, for example eating well and sleeping enough. If you're worried about your flow for any reason, consider discussing this with your grown-up (see pages 178–182 for more on period problems).

HOW LONG WILL MY PERIOD LAST?

Everyone is different, but most people get their periods for around three to five days, sometimes slightly less, or sometimes a little longer.

HOW OFTEN WILL I GET MY PERIOD?

This can vary from person to person, but on average, periods come every 29.3 days – or once a month! There is more about this on page 122.

WHAT IF MY PERIOD DOESN'T COME?

Almost all girls will start their period by the time they are 16. A very tiny number may not menstruate due to medical reasons such as anatomy, low body weight or hormones. If you are worried about your period not starting, it's always good to talk to a trusted adult.

ONCE MY PERIOD STARTS, WILL I GET IT EVERY MONTH . . . LIKE . . . FOREVER?!

No. Periods usually stop if a woman is pregnant and often, especially if their baby is breastfed, they take a while to start again. Otherwise, periods come roughly once a month until you are around 50 years old. At this point, they slow down and stop during a time in your life called the menopause. After the menopause happens, women can't have babies any more. Fifty might sound massively old to you right now, but actually, when you get there, it won't *feel* very old at all, and you will still have another whole phase of your life *after* your periods stop happening.

★ STILL WORRIED? ★ LET'S BUST SOME MYTHS!

You might have heard rumours about periods that have made you worry. But what if the stuff you've picked up in the school corridors is not 100 per cent accurate?! Let's take the most common period myths and bust them!

★ MYTH 1: There will be LOADS of BLOOD!

Well, first of all, as you have read on page 39, periods are not just blood! You might be told that every period will be roughly 30 to 50 ml of period blood (or two to three tablespoons), but that's not really the full picture. Your period also contains the lining of your uterus (which looks pretty much like blood, but technically, it's something different!). With the blood and the lining combined, *over your whole period* you might lose more like 80 to 100 ml of period blood.

TO GIVE YOU A VISUAL PICTURE, 100 ML =

SIX AND A HALF TABLESPOONS

ABOUT A THIRD OF A CAN OF FIZZY DRINK

TWO-THIRDS OF THE TEA IN AN OLD-FASHIONED TEACUP

And remember – that's over the course of the *whole* period which lasts on average three to five days.

However, as you know if you've ever knocked over your nearly empty glass of squash, even a small amount of liquid can seem like a big spillage! Just a teaspoon or two of period blood can look like a lot more! Don't panic, remember it's not as much as it looks, and if it really *does* feel like a lot, or you are at all worried, speak to your grown-up or ask another adult you trust for help.

✦ MYTH 2: It's AGONY!

Good news – your first period might not hurt at all or you might experience uncomfortable, 'crampy' feelings. Going forwards, you might have periods that are not at all painful, or you might have one or two days each month where you have pain or cramps. However, this pain should not be severe enough to keep you off school or prevent you from doing your usual activities. Severe pain could be a sign that something isn't right. For more about 'period pain' see pages 178–82.

✦ MYTH 3: Everyone will know

You will hopefully feel very excited about starting your period, and want to tell your mum, dad or other special adults in your life. You may also like sharing the news with your friends – perhaps they have already started and you have been waiting to join the Period Gang! Or maybe you are the first and founding member, a very special honour!

However, unless you tell them, *nobody will know if you have your period*. You won't look any different, and you should be able to participate in any activity you wish, just like normal. You can take your time to tell people, and maybe have a while to think about what's happened first. Who you tell, when you tell them, and how you tell them, is completely

Up. To. You.

And you definitely don't have to tell your maths teacher or the boy at the back of the class! Only tell the people who you want to tell.

✷ MYTH 4: You're a woman now

When you start your period, sometimes people will tell you that

now you are a woman

95

as if that special Fairy Godmother showed up again with the first drop of period blood, tapped you with a wand and magically transformed you! But of course, in reality, growing up is a very gradual process, and your menarche is just one small part of it. Sure, getting your period is one sign that you are moving from child to adult, but it also doesn't just change who you are overnight. You are still the same person you were before it started, and you are allowed to keep enjoying your 'childhood' in the ways that you were, if you want to.

It's also important to remember that becoming a woman doesn't mean you have to behave or dress in a certain way. Women can have long hair or short hair, wear lots of make-up or none. They can dress how they like and do any job or play any sport. There are no rules and how you express yourself is completely up to you.

The Mirror

Take time each day to say hello to your reflection in the mirror. You can do this when you wash your hands, clean your teeth or any time you are in the bathroom or near another mirror. Pause for a moment and make eye contact with yourself. Tell your reflection something positive, such as, 'Guess who did great in their maths test!' or 'You were a great friend today!'. Then tell yourself, 'You are an amazing and beautiful person', 'You are good enough' or 'You are brave and strong.' Think of other nice things to say to your reflection, and get in the habit of saying them in your head, or even out loud, each time you look in a mirror.

★ TALKING TO GROWN-UPS ABOUT PERIODS ★

'I'VE STARTED!!!!!' At some point, you're going to have to say these two little words to your grown-up, so it's a good idea to think about *how*. You might have a very relaxed family who talk openly about lots of things or you might not.

The fact is – some grown-ups might feel a bit awkward talking about periods! This is because, when they were growing up, there was a lot more pressure on people to keep quiet about menstrual stuff. And even though that's started to change, it's still a subject that some feel a bit shy about.

It's really good to talk to grown-ups you trust about periods – they will probably have some helpful information and maybe even some funny stories for you. They might start the conversation, but if they don't, why not be the one who is first to show you are not embarrassed to talk about this?

Here's some tips:

★ If you can, get chatting about periods before you get your first one. If you talk about periods and puberty with your grown-ups before your first period happens, this will make it much easier to tell them when it happens.

★ Keep it casual! Try just asking a little question on a car journey or when you are snuggled up watching TV.

★ Something like an advert or a story line in a programme might help you get started, and ask something like, 'Grown-up, what was it like when you got *your* first period?'

★ Don't leave out dads! Your dad or other male grown-up will have had lots of experiences with periods, and might be really touched that you have included them.

★ If you don't feel you can talk to either of your parents, try to find another grown-up that you trust, such as a big sister, aunt, your favourite teacher or neighbour.

★ Use this book! Say, 'Mum, Dad ... have you heard of Rupi Kaur?!' (see pages 200-202). You can then impress them by starting a family discussion about why people get so freaked out by period blood – but not other blood for example, and maybe discuss some of the other amazing things you have learned, too.

Pssst ... if you need to talk to a different grown-up about having your period, for example you need to tell a teacher that you can't or don't feel like joining in a sports activity or swim session, or you need to mention your period to a doctor, remember – they are a professional and it's OK! They will understand and will have had this conversation with lots of girls before you. Even though you might feel awkward, they definitely don't. So be brave and just say it.

★ OVER THE MOON! ★
CELEBRATING YOUR FIRST PERIOD

In lots of different places around the world, getting your first period is a cause for celebration. **IN BRAZIL,** girls from the Amazonian Ticuna tribe spend between three months and a year, living in a private room in their house when they get their first period. This time is called the **Pelazón** and girls are taught about their tribe's history, music and beliefs before being welcomed back into their community with great celebration.

IN NORTH AMERICA, the Apache tribe have an elaborate ritual called **The Sunrise Ceremony**, where girls spend four days and nights in a special outfit, dancing and running to show strength, singing, enacting the story of the Changing Woman, sharing special foods and celebrating her transition to womanhood.

IN CANADA, a tribe called the Nuuchahnulth celebrate by taking the young woman out to sea – her

100

101

whole village watches and cheers for her as she swims
back to the shore.

IN SOUTH INDIA,

in a ceremony called
Ritu Kala Samskara, young
girls are given a special party,
with flower garlands, gifts
and a special outfit to wear
for the first time called
a 'half sari'.

IN JAPAN, first periods are celebrated by the family
eating a special dish called **Sekihan**, made of rice and
red beans.

If you are not from a culture where something like this happens, it might sound strange to you to celebrate getting your first period. But you might find it really nice to just do *something*, even something small to mark the occasion. Here are some suggestions:

★ pampering session with besties
★ trying out make-up
★ a trip to the cinema
★ run a new distance
★ a swim in a river or the sea (with an adult to keep you safe)
★ create a spa day in your bathroom
★ eating lots of chocolate
★ having your favourite food for tea
★ trying something new you've always wanted to try
★ starting a new diary
★ writing a story or a poem
★ duvet day with your favourite movies
★ dressing up in red
★ manicure or pedicure with red nail polish.

★ GETTING READY: ★ CREATING A FIRST PERIOD KIT

This is a really fun activity that can help you feel ready for your very first period! The idea is to just pack a minimal kit in case your first period starts when you are out and about, at school or on a trip for example.

HERE'S WHAT YOU NEED TO GATHER TOGETHER:

✦ A BAG

This doesn't have to be big – around 20 cm by 15 cm should do, although if you want to include spare leggings, for example, it might need to be a bit bigger. You could think about making this if you are crafty or upcycling an old bag. Pop this bag inside your school bag and keep it there all the time so you know where it is when you need it most.

✦ YOUR PERIOD PRODUCT

The most important thing in your bag is the product you think you are most likely to want to use for your first-ever period. Two pads (disposable or reusable) OR a pair of period underwear OR your menstrual cup OR a couple of tampons OR another product. If there's room, it's nice to put a spare pad or tampon in there to help a friend in need, too!

✦ WIPES

You might want or need to clean yourself if your first period takes you by surprise, so pack some wipes. You can buy packs of individually wrapped wipes which are useful because they are lighter and easier to fit in your bag. For an eco-alternative, you can buy reusable cloth wipes which you then need to take home in a 'wet bag' after use (see page 106).

✦ SPARE UNDERWEAR

Your first period will probably get on the knickers you are wearing, so pack a spare pair of underwear so that you can get changed and feel fresh. If you want to, you can also roll up a pair of leggings or shorts in case your period gets on your outer layer of clothing.

★ WET BAG

This is something to put your used knickers or used cloth pads in. A standard plastic freezer bag will do or a smaller cloth bag. Some reusable pad companies sell special 'wet bags', which are a little bag made of waterproof, washable material that you can put any used cloth wipes, cloth pads or period pants into. This will keep everything safe until it can be put in the laundry.

★ A TREAT!

Why not also put in something special to save for that very special day when your first period arrives? How about one of the following:

- ☑ A mini bar of your favourite chocolate
- ☑ A brand-new lip balm in an exciting flavour
- ☑ A smart new pen or pencil to take into your next lesson
- ☑ A necklace or bracelet that means something to you

Your mum, dad or another grown-up might want to put something in to your first period kit, too. Perhaps they might like to write you a special note, sealed in an envelope ONLY to be opened when you start?!

Psssst ... Once you've had your first period, you'll still need a period kit to keep in your bag. Your first year or two of periods can be irregular (see page 122), so it's good to be prepared! Most women and girls keep some kind of period product in their handbag, so they're not caught out. If this does ever happen to you, don't worry, we've all forgotten to repack supplies ...

STUCK WITHOUT YOUR PERIOD KIT?

What do you do if your period starts and you don't have anything you need with you?

★ TIP 1 - VENDING MACHINES

Some public toilets have vending machines selling single pads or tampons. If you've got some change with you, this could be an option.

★ TIP 2 - ASK FOR HELP!

If you are in a public toilet or the school toilets, it's OK to ask another woman or girl for help. They will be really pleased to help you out and they will almost certainly have been in the same situation and got help from a stranger themselves at some point. Just say, 'Excuse me, I've just got my period and I've not got a pad – do you have anything?'

★ TIP 3 - MAKE A WEDGE!

This is an old trick that girls have been doing for years! Just roll up several layers of toilet paper and put this in your underwear until you can get home or to a shop. If you're worried that the wedge will fall out of your knickers, you could push the top of it gently inside your labia and encourage it to stick. It might not work for the netball match or the disco, but it will do in an emergency!

Cycle Superstars!

MARY KENNER

Inventor

Mary Kenner was born in 1912 in North Carolina, USA.
Even when she was a little girl, she already had an
incredible skill – when she saw a problem, she would
straight away start figuring out ways to solve it. If
something didn't work properly, rather than getting
frustrated, Mary would see this as a chance to improve

the world she lived in. For example, when a door kept squeaking, she set to work thinking about how you could make a hinge that could oil itself! When she noticed how rainwater dripped off an umbrella and onto the floor, she invented a sponge that attached to the umbrella tip to stop this happening.

So, of course, when it came to periods, Mary could see there was huge room for improvement! At the time, women were still using simple rags and cloth pads, but Mary got busy and invented the 'Sanitary Belt', an adjustable belt to wear during your period, with a built-in pocket for the absorbent pad.

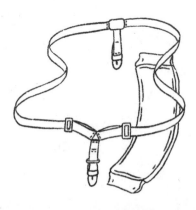

In 1956 Mary got a 'patent' for her belt – a special way of making sure that nobody can copy your design. This was difficult and expensive for her to do, but it looked like it would pay off when a big company showed an interest in her invention. However, because Mary was African-American, and because, at the time, people with black skin were treated very badly, the company decided not to work with her. Her patent then expired, meaning that anybody could use the design for her belt, and it became very popular – although Mary herself never made any money from it.

Mary was not put off. She kept inventing for the rest of her life, and filed more patents than any other African-American woman in history! Her sanitary belt was widely used until the 1980s, and she died in 2006 at the age of 94.

★ MENSTRUAL MERCH! ★

Just like Mary Kenner's belt, new period products just keep being invented, and they don't start and end with pads! There is a growing number of interesting and fun period stuff to buy as well! For example:

✦ PERIOD JEWELLERY

From subtle red gemstone bracelets to full on earrings in the shape of bloody tampons and pads, you can find all kinds of period jewellery, badges and pins online. They're a good way to celebrate your period.

✦ PERIOD SUBSCRIPTION BOXES

You might have already had a subscription box of craft ideas or science projects – but what's more obvious for your menstrual cycle than a monthly box? You'll get cloth pads, disposable pads, tampons or a selection sent to you each month, often organic, sometimes with extra treats like chocolate in the box and often with built in donations to help fight period poverty (see page 65).

✦ PERIOD TECH

Period gadgets are the future (and perhaps YOU will invent the next one?!). From 'smart' cups and tampons that tell you when they are full and track your period, to pain relieving pulsers that you clip to your underwear and apps and fitness trackers that help track your cycle, the range of menstrual machines just keeps on growing!

(Still no news on the gizmo that brings you a duvet and a pizza JUST when you need it though!)

Cycle Superstars!

ARUNACHALAM MURUGANANTHAM

 'Pad Man'

Arunachalam grew up in poverty in India and left school at the age of 14. One day he was watching his wife collecting newspapers and rags for her period because they could not afford pads. Like many inventors, he thought, 'There must be a better way'. He set to work trying to figure out how to make pads that his wife and other women like her could easily afford. Lots of people laughed at Arunachalam for being so interested in periods, and even his wife and sisters refused to help

him. He even had to test out the pads by wearing them himself! Eventually, though, he invented a low-cost machine that could make pads, and took it to a big presentation in Mumbai, where it won an award and funding. Instead of selling his invention to make money, Arunachalam chose to provide his machines to groups of women on low incomes. And the rest is history. Arunachalam's pad-making machine has changed the lives of many women in rural India, creating jobs for them making pads, and ensuring they have pads for themselves so they can keep working during their periods.

Arunachalam's story is so amazing that lots of people have made films and documentaries about him. Some people even call him 'Pad Man', which is the name of the big Bollywood movie about his life.

What period product could YOU invent?

CHAPTER FIVE

Super Splendiferous Cycles

CHAPTER FIVE

Super Splendiferous Cycles

When it comes to puberty, periods tend to take centre stage!

But there is more – **MUCH MORE** – to all this than just periods!

Periods are just one small part of your

MENSTRUAL CYCLE.

When people give you the 'puberty chat' they quite often talk a lot about periods, but this book is here to tell you that a whole **HEAP** of useful information is left out if we just think about the four or five days a month when we get our periods. Yes, it's really important to learn all about them, that's true. But what's even more important is to understand that you don't just have a **PERIOD** each month. Each month you have a **MENSTRUAL CYCLE**.

A cycle just means something that goes round and round on repeat. Like the wheel of your bike.

✦ THERE'S THE CYCLE OF THE SEASONS.

Spring, summer, autumn, winter, repeat!

✦ OR THE CYCLE OF THE DAY.

Sunrise, morning, midday, afternoon, evening, sunset, night-time, repeat!

120

✦ OR HAVE YOU HEARD OF THE LUNAR CYCLE?

You might not know all the names for the phases of the Moon, but you've probably seen the Moon make different shapes in the sky. It does this in a cycle. *New moon, waxing crescent, first quarter, waxing gibbous, full moon, waning gibbous, last quarter, waning crescent, repeat!*

OK – you get the idea! So each month you have a **MENSTRUAL CYCLE**. (Menstrual just means 'monthly' but it normally applies to all things period related!)

Each stage of your menstrual cycle has a different name – *period – follicular phase – ovulation – luteal phase ... repeat!*

THE FULL SPIN ON YOUR CYCLE!

A menstrual cycle usually lasts 26 to 30 days, but it
can be shorter or longer, and especially during the first
few years of your period, it's normal to have longer
cycles, meaning that you won't necessarily see a period
each month as you might expect. You might also have
'irregular' cycle lengths throughout your life, which
sometimes last less than 21 days or as many as 45 days
and vary each month. Lots of people think that, once
you've been having periods for a few years, the 'right'
length of a cycle is 28 days, but this isn't really accurate.
On average the menstrual cycle is thought to be 29.3
days, but it's not 'wrong' to be a bit shorter or longer
than this.

Your cycle has two big features – your period, which
you've now read quite a lot about, and ovulation, which
is pretty amazing and is coming up next. But there are
names for the rest of your monthly cycle too. As you'll
see from the cycle diagram opposite, your month is
divided into a **follicular phase** and a **luteal phase**.

PERIOD Well you hopefully know what that is by now! If no egg has been fertilised, the lining of your uterus comes away and comes out of your vagina. Everyone's different, but this takes up about 5 days of your cycle.

FOLLICULAR PHASE This is the name for the time from the start of your period to when you ovulate, and it lasts about two weeks on average. A hormone called FSH (Follicle Stimulating Hormone) causes the eggs in the follicles of your ovaries to mature and get ready to be released.

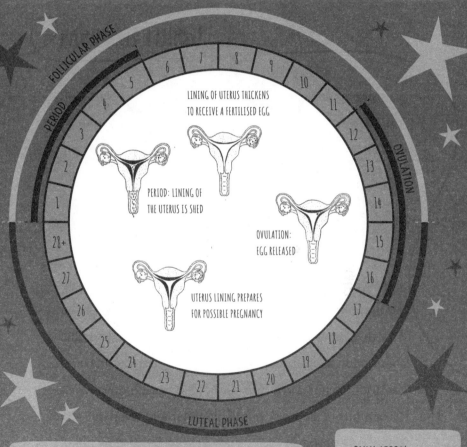

FOLLICULAR PHASE

PERIOD

OVULATION

LUTEAL PHASE

LINING OF UTERUS THICKENS TO RECEIVE A FERTILISED EGG

PERIOD: LINING OF THE UTERUS IS SHED

OVULATION: EGG RELEASED

UTERUS LINING PREPARES FOR POSSIBLE PREGNANCY

1 2 3 4 5 6 7 8 9 10 11 12 13 14 15 16 17 18 19 20 21 22 23 24 25 26 27 28+

LUTEAL PHASE After you've ovulated, another hormone, progesterone, kicks in and gets the lining of your uterus ready for the egg. This phase lasts roughly two weeks, at which point, if the egg is not fertilised, the lining of your uterus begins to break down, and hey presto, it's period time again! And round and round we go in our cycle!

OVULATION One egg (and sometimes two) is released. In an average cycle, this happens around Day 14.

Hmmm....had enough of the biology lesson ? I know – *progesterone* ... *luteal* ... how do you even *say* some of these words?!

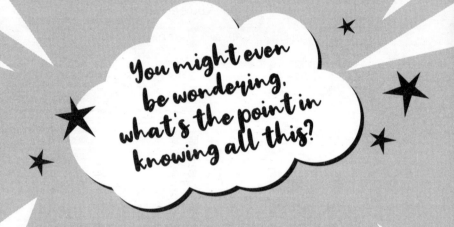

You might even be wondering, what's the point in knowing all this?

Well, when you are much older, if you decide to be a doctor or a scientist, or if you want to have a baby or *avoid* having a baby, it will be really useful to know this stuff. But it's also really fantastic to know about it *now*, because all these phases of your cycle start happening to you during puberty and when you start your periods. And, amazingly, they can have a really **BIG** affect on **YOU**, how you **FEEL**, what you want to **DO** with your time and what you **NEED**.

And once you understand *that*, then you can start to notice how *your* menstrual cycle affects you personally – and everyone is different! By tuning in to YOUR cycle and how it makes **YOU** feel, you can learn to look after yourself better by listening to your body, trusting your body and loving your body. In other words, you can become a

CYCLE DETECTIVE!

BECOMING A CYCLE DETECTIVE!

Earlier on, in Chapter 2, we thought about ways you could tune in to your body and pick up any secret signals of when your first period might come. But this is just the first step to becoming a Cycle Detective! Once your period starts, you can keep listening in to the signs your body is giving you, from your flow to your feelings, and even to the fluid in your knickers, and get vital clues about your overall health. This can help you to understand and look after yourself better. This is very important –

because

YOU
are very
important!

As a Cycle Detective, you need to know that your body is unique and that your own signs and signals will be special and different from other people's. The best way to tune in is to remember to listen to your body, trust your body, and love your body!

LISTEN TO YOUR BODY

Even though you might not realise it, I bet you are already a real expert at listening to your body. For example, you know when you are hungry, right? Or thirsty? Or tired? Your body tells you these things, and you *listen*. Your period will bring you a new way to listen to your body. As a Cycle Detective, you can start noticing the signs and clues your body gives you throughout the month. While your menstrual cycles may vary for the first few years, over time you will tune in to your cycle and start to get a picture of what's normal for you and your body. Listen out for changes, which can be messages from your body that you need to rest, eat nutritious foods, sleep more or even see a doctor. A big part of it is *trusting* your body.

TRUST YOUR BODY

Cycle Detectives need to follow their hunches, listen carefully to the clues and trust the coded messages!

Your body knows what it's doing. Have confidence in it. Part of growing up is about really getting to know your body, listening to what it has to tell you and trusting the messages it gives you. If you are thirsty, drink! If you need to move, move! And if you need help, ask for help.

YOUR BODY IS CLEVER, STRONG AND *amazing!*

♀ LOVE YOUR BODY

So, you are *listening* to your body and *trusting* your body. There's only one more thing you need to do – **LOVE** your body! Being a Cycle Detective will help you to notice the times each month when your body needs a bit of extra love. Love for your body comes in all different forms. Sometimes it's the food you eat, sometimes the activities you choose and sometimes it's even the thoughts you think.

> *Your body is like your own special house that you get to live in for an entire lifetime. It makes sense to look after it! And it makes sense to be proud of it, and to love it, too.*

And, if you're going to start noticing what's happening in your body more, Cycle Detectives, there's one really show-stopping event in your cycle that you absolutely need to know more about. In fact, it might be even more fantastic than your period, it's....

OVULATION!

THE OVULATION CELEBRATION!

Ovulation, as you've already read on page 123, is when an egg is released by one of your ovaries and makes its way down the fallopian tube (see page 37) where it waits to be fertilised.

You normally only release one egg during your menstrual cycle, and it can come from either ovary. Occasionally, a second egg will sneak out too, and that's one way that twins can happen!

Your eggs are *tiny* – about 0.1 mm. That's still visible to the naked eye – but titchy – about the size of the full stop at the end of this sentence.

★ EGG-STRAVAGANZA! ★

Did you know that you were *born* with all your eggs?! Over a MILLION of them?!

And that even when you were in your mum's uterus (womb), you already had all of those eggs – in fact, you had even more then, as many as 7 million?! And (get ready to be mind blown), when your mum was in her mum's uterus, SHE had all HER eggs too! Okey dokey, have you worked out what that means yet? Yup ... think about it ... think about it ... keep thinking ...

HOLY GUACAMOLE!
The egg that went on to become YOU was
INSIDE YOUR MATERNAL GRANDMA!

Even more amazingly, our egg cells contain something called 'mitochondrial DNA', genetic codes that only pass from mother to child. This means that all humans can be traced back genetically through the female line of their family, sometimes called their 'matrilineage' or 'motherline'.

Isn't it interesting to think that we are all connected in this way through one long and never-ending line of mothers and grandmothers and great grandmothers? Even if your mum or parent is not your biological relation, for example, if you were adopted, you still have this line of connection back through the whole of human history. And of course, if you go on to have children, and they go on to have children – YOUR grandchildren will have come from eggs which were once inside YOU!

Yes, I know. Fascinating!!

WHEN DO I OVULATE?

Some people think that you *always* ovulate in the middle of your cycle, half way through or around about Day 14. However, it's also normal to ovulate earlier or later in your cycle than this. When you ovulate is not *fixed* – it might vary or you may even skip a month because you are in the first few years of having your periods and your cycle is just getting established, or because you have been ill, stressed or run down.

What is *more* fixed is the time between ovulation happening and the first day of your period. Once you have *definitely* ovulated, you *will* very likely start your period between a minimum of 12 and a maximum of 16 days later. So – get ready to be amazed –

if you get to know when you ovulate, you will get to have a much better idea of when to expect your period.

★ OVULATION INVESTIGATION ★

It's obvious when you have your period – you bleed! But did you know that some women can tell when they are ovulating? Well, Cycle Detectives, your body will often give you some signs! And the more cycles you have, the better you will get at spotting them!

✦ CLUE 1: EGG WHITE EVIDENCE

There's more about your vaginal fluids on pages 155–158, but when it comes to ovulating you need to know that the stuff you find in your knickers is likely to be a bit like raw egg white – slippery and stretchy between your fingers.

✦ CLUE 2: TELL-TALE TWINGES

Sometimes when you ovulate you might feel a little twinge, ache or mild pain in one side of your lower tummy, which doesn't last long and is not severe. If you do feel this sensation, it will be on the side of your body with the ovary that's ovulating.

✦ CLUE 3: SPOT THE SPOTS

You might experience a few tiny spots of blood in your underwear around the time you ovulate, due to the changes in your hormones. This is nothing to worry about, but if you are concerned, speak to a grown-up you trust. And while we are talking about spotting spots, you might find that you get a few extra pimples on your face around ovulation – and you can blame your hormones for that, too!

✦ CLUE 4: TEMPERATURE TIP-OFFS

This clue is a bit more complex and requires you to use a digital thermometer to take your temperature, each morning, when you first wake up. You can then record your temperature, just by jotting it down on a piece of paper or, if you prefer, on a chart or graph. Over time, you'll notice that something very *interesting* happens to your temperature when you ovulate – it rises by 0.2 degrees Celsius or more! It can be quite fun to track your temperature, but if it feels a bit complicated, you don't need to.

✦ CLUE 5: FEELING FAB

Some women and girls even find that, around the time of ovulation, they feel super energetic, full of ideas and even more confident than they do at other times in their cycle.

✦ YOUR OWN SECRET SIGNALS

In time you may also get to know *your own* clues. When *your* body ovulates, you might notice other things about your body or how you feel. Sometimes you might not notice anything, and that's fine too. As you listen to your body, you will learn to trust its clues.

And remember, if you *are* able to notice your ovulation, that from the day that you ovulate, you can count down 12 to 16 days until you *know* you will get your period.

HIGH5

Make a list of the top FIVE things you like or love about your body. Some of these might be to do with how you look and others might be to do with your body's abilities, for example, 'fast runner', 'dance champion', etc. Try making other High5s, your High5 of things you are good at, High5 foods, High5 school subjects, High5 of things you are wishing for, High5 of things you would like to do when you grow up ... and as many other High5s as you can think of.

TUNING INTO YOUR CYCLE

As you get better and better at Cycle Detection, you will start to notice more and more about your cycle and how it affects you. To begin with, you might just detect when your period is coming, or when you might be ovulating, but as you get better at noticing the clues, you may find you build up a clearer and clearer picture of your journey through your cycle. Remember, this will be different for everyone and unique to you! But you might find that you notice changes in yourself, your moods, your energy and what you most feel like doing as you go through each menstrual cycle.

And this knowledge can be like a magic key, unlocking a much better understanding of yourself!

For example, some research suggests *ovulation* is a time when you feel full of energy, ideas and confidence. And you could make this work to your advantage! Another time in your cycle that can be really powerful is the week before you get your period. At this time, it's common to feel things more intensely and you might feel upset, tearful, emotional or just plain out **MAD**. People might tell you that this is *'only hormones'* but just because hormones are making you feel things more *deeply*, this definitely doesn't mean your feelings are just made up! Instead of thinking of this time in a negative way, you could think of it as a chance to focus on what you need, what you want, and what you wish was different. This might be something about your own life (for example a friend that isn't being kind to you) or something about the world that you don't think is fair and want to change. Again, this is another chance to tune into yourself, listen to the clues, and, just like all good detectives, follow all your hunches!

Pssst ... some people call the time before their period PMT or Premenstrual TENSION. However, others say the T stands for TRUTH, because it's a time when we see things – especially the tough stuff – more clearly. Some months, it's like a really bright light gets shone on the dark corners of our lives that we usually ignore. This can help us make improvements. Enjoy your Premenstrual Truth!!

But what about the week when you actually get your period? How will you feel then, and what will you need?

Well, it depends on you, although lots of girls do find that, for at least the first couple of days of their period, they feel the need to slow down a bit and rest. Other people find that their energy levels are just the same, or that they feel better if they move, do sport, or carry on with things as they normally do. And sometimes it can be different every month, so it's all about listening to your body.

To help you get an even better picture of the different phases of the menstrual cycle, some people like to think of it as being a bit like the four seasons ...

FOUR SEASONS – NO, IT'S NOT A PIZZA!

Yes, I know that Four Seasons might be one of your favourite pizza flavours ... or maybe you prefer Hawaiian? But sorry, this is not about melted cheese, it's just another way of thinking about the different phases of your cycle each month and the different types of energy you might have as it goes round.

Just like a Four Seasons pizza, your cycle has four different sections (and just like a pizza, some sections may melt and overlap into each other a bit!). Thinking about the different phases of each cycle as 'seasons' can help you tune in more to how you might be feeling, what activities you might like doing and even what kind of food you might feel like eating. There are some suggestions below – but yours might be different of course!

✦ SPRING

This is the time just after your period, the follicular phase, when you may start to feel more energetic. You know that brilliant time of year when you see new leaves on the trees and the daffodils all come up? The sun is shining and you suddenly get loads of brilliant new ideas. You don't need your coat and you can skip along in your favourite T-shirt feeling really light and excited! This is what this part of your cycle can feel like.

☑ **FEELING:** Optimistic, energised, fresh
☑ **FOOD:** Fruit salad, crunchy carrot sticks, raspberry meringues

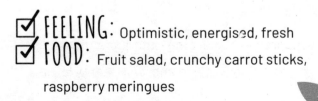

☑ ACTIVITY: Planning a new project, starting a new hobby, having a massive bedroom tidy!

✦ SUMMER

This is the 'prime time' you might experience when you ovulate. It's as if all the flowers are out now and you can freewheel down hills on your bike, dance under the stars or hit the beach with your besties! There's no school and the holiday will last forever! Everything is blooming! This can be how it feels around the time we ovulate.

☑ FEELING: Powerful, strong, healthy

☑ FOOD: Homemade ice lollies, tuna and cucumber sandwiches, Victoria sponge cake

☑ ACTIVITY: bodyboarding in the sea, netball goal practice, running for a role on your school council, taking selfies with your bff

✦ AUTUMN

This is your premenstrual time – the 'luteal' phase – when everything slows down and your energy levels might drop. It's like those crisp days when the leaves are falling from the trees, crops are being harvested and ripe fruit is being picked. You get to see what's been grown during the energetic spring and summer, and you 'take stock'. Maybe it's been a good harvest and you feel calm and satisfied, or maybe you feel frustrated, grumpy and disappointed. These can be some of the feelings of the time in the run up to your period.

☑ **FEELING:** Sad, overwhelmed, reflective

☑ **FOOD:** Apple slices dipped in nut butter, tomato soup with melted cheese, chicken pie

☑ **ACTIVITY:** Writing a journal, talking with friends, signing or planning a petition

✦ WINTER

This is the time when you have your period. Imagine it's cold outside, the snow is falling, so you shut the door on the world, light candles or a crackling log fire and hide under your duvet! You just want to snuggle up, watch box sets or soppy movies or just stare at your phone or out of the window, as you wait for the energy and warmth of spring to return. This might be how you feel around the days when your period arrives.

 FEELING: Dreamy, sleepy, disconnected
 FOOD: Buttery baked potatoes, toasted cheese sandwiches, warm chocolate brownies

ACTIVITY: Duvet days, writing letters or emails, baking cakes, eating comfort food

As you cycle through these four seasons with each menstrual cycle, you will get to know each one better and what it's like for you. You will learn how each season typically makes you feel, what you need most in each phase, what foods you crave and what activities suit you best at each time. You might discover when is the best time to tackle situations you are not happy about, when it's best to start new projects and when in your cycle you have the most interesting dreams, see things more clearly and have plans and visions for your future.

IT'S A WAY OF GETTING TO KNOW YOURSELF.

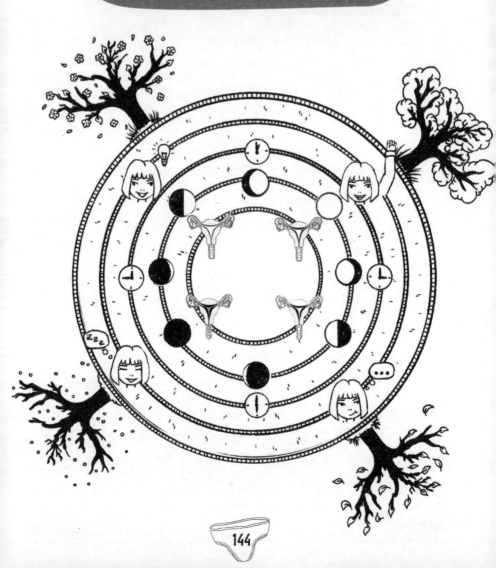

LOOK HOW YOUR CYCLE FITS INTO NOT JUST THE SEASONS, BUT SO MANY OTHER CYCLES!

144

★ PERIODS AND THE MOON ★

You might have heard that women's cycles are connected to the Moon – but is this true?

Well, it certainly IS true that the lunar cycle is 29.5 days, which is also very close to the length of the average menstrual cycle, thought to be 29.3 days. However, research into over 7.5 million women's cycles by the menstrual-tracking app Clue found that women didn't synchronise up with the Moon's phases in any kind of pattern. Of course – some women's cycles WILL match up with these lunar events – but many scientists think this is just down to coincidence.

HOWEVER! Some people wonder WHY our cycles are the same length as the Moon's cycle, and if it's more than just a coincidence. And we don't really know the answer. What we do know is that all light, including moonlight, has an effect on our body's production of the hormone melatonin, which can affect our menstrual cycles. And a long time ago, before we had electric light, the changes in light levels caused by the phases of the Moon would have had a much stronger impact on our melatonin – so maybe, just maybe, in the days before lightbulbs and mobile phone screens, we were more in sync with our silvery sister in the sky.

CHAPTER SIX

Charting Your Cycles

CHAPTER SIX
Charting Your Cycles

GET TRACKING, CYCLE DETECTIVES!

Your cycle will be unique and special, just like you are. Some of you might feel like hibernating during your period, whilst others will be full of the joys of spring. Books like this one are only a guide. The point is to get to know what **YOUR** cycle is like for **YOU**.

Other stuff apart from your periods will also affect how you feel. Each day, each month and each year of your life will have ups and downs, good times and bad times, struggles and triumphs.

You are much, MUCH more than just your menstrual cycle!

However, your menstrual cycle is **ONE** way to explore who you are and take care of yourself. It's a way to listen to, trust and love your body.

And one brilliant way of listening to your body more carefully is to

TRACK YOUR CYCLE.

This basically means making a note each day of what is happening with your period or fluids, your feelings and your energy. You can use a chart, **like this example** on the page opposite, to keep a track of how you feel each month.

Psssst ... You don't have to have started your periods to track your cycle. Although you don't have a menstrual cycle, you will still probably notice changes in your body and your feelings over the month, and as well as helping you to learn how to listen to your body, it might also give you more clues about when your menstrual cycle will start.

Cycle Chart

EMOTIONS: ☺ ☹ ☹ ☹

FLOW/FLUIDS: SPOT LIGHT MEDIUM HEAVY NONE EGG-WHITE STICKY, WET

ENERGY: ↑ ↓ —

My Cycle Chart

Trace a copy of the blank cycle chart below every month to track your own cycle, or download a printable PDF of this at: https://geni.us/MyPeriodCycleChart

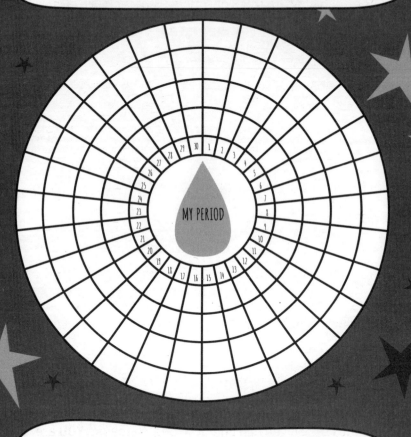

MONTH/YEAR:

OTHER NOTES:

HOW TO USE THE CHART

Use each chart to track one menstrual cycle, always starting a new chart on the first day of your period. If your cycle lasts longer than 30 days simply start a new chart and finish tracking that cycle on the new chart. Then start another new chart on the first day of your next period.

If you don't have a cycle yet, just start when you feel ready and track how you feel for 30 days.

Write the date each day in the outermost ring of the chart.

On each chart you are going to record three key pieces of information: your **FLOW** (including any vaginal **FLUIDS**), your **FEELINGS** and your **ENERGY**. Don't worry if you miss a day or two, and remember your chart is all about **YOU**, so you can't get it wrong – because **YOU** are the expert on yourself!

YOUR FLOW

During your period, track your flow each day. During the rest of the month, track your vaginal fluids (more on that in a mo!) in the same section of the chart.

Your flow will be Spot, L, M, or H. Spot is for spotting, which sometimes happens for a day or two before your period officially starts or when you ovulate and you will notice small drops of period blood or rust-coloured vaginal fluid in your underwear. You can write 'Spot' or draw a 'dot' for this one. L is for light flow, M is for medium flow and H is for heavy flow. It's up to you to decide which of these best describes your own flow. One person's medium flow might be somebody else's heavy flow, and that's OK.

☆ REMEMBER – YOU CAN'T GET IT WRONG! ☆

Your vaginal fluids will be N for none, S for sticky, E for egg white or W for wet (see pages 156-157 for more information).

Each day the Flow section should contain a letter to show your period or vaginal fluids, or N for none. You will soon get to remember what the different letters mean!

FABULOUS FLUIDS!

So, Cycle Detectives, you already know that when you ovulate, one of the signs can be an 'egg white' type fluid in your knickers. But, there's more knowledge to be had here, and if you start paying attention to other fluids you find in your underwear, you're going to get even more clues about what's happening in your cycle.

Vaginal fluid is rather clever stuff. It's actually mostly produced by your cervix (see page 37), and is sometimes also called cervical fluid. You might find reading about this a bit strange, but really, it's not, because it happens to everyone! Even the female pop stars and celebrities you like have vaginal fluid, although not all of them will know as much about it as you will by the time you reach the end of this section!

Your amazing cervix produces different fluid depending on where you are in your cycle, so learning a bit about these different types can give you more clues, in particular to when you are ovulating – and this can give you a clearer idea when to expect your period.

You can get to know your vaginal fluid in two main ways. You can simply notice it in your knickers (or on the toilet paper when you wipe). Or you can use your fingers to feel the different types of fluid you find in your vagina at different times of the month.

Whichever way feels best for you, you might notice that you have different types of fluid and that it comes in different consistencies. You might notice that it sometimes even bleaches the colour of your darker underwear. If you like, you can record what you notice in your cycle chart (using the letters N, S, W, or E) as well as your period flow (Spot, L, M, H).

During your menstrual cycle, there might be, in order of appearance after your period ends, the following:

✦ N – NONE

No fluid at all. This is most often the case in the first few days after your period. Your underwear doesn't have anything to show you, and if you touch your vulva or vagina, it might feel dry or only very slightly moist.

✦ S – STICKY

Next up comes this stuff which is sticky and tacky when moist, and when it dries in your underwear, slightly crumbly. It is usually white, yellow or opaque.

✦ W – WET

As you get closer to ovulation, your cervical fluid becomes more like lotion: watery and thin. It can be slippery at first and then and start to get creamier as you get closer to ovulation. It can be whitish or cloudy and yellowish as it dries on your underwear.

✦ E – EGG WHITE

This is the stuff that arrives around the time that you are ovulating, and lots of people say it's like raw egg white, well, because that's a pretty accurate description really!

If you get some between your fingers it will stretch, just like egg white does, sometimes for several centimetres. After you've ovulated, and you enter the luteal phase, your fluid will usually go back to being Sticky or None, until your period arrives, and off we go on the cycle again ...

NOT SUCH FABULOUS FLUIDS – WHEN TO WORRY

Getting to know what's normal for you will help you to keep track of your vaginal health and know when and if something isn't right. Usually your fluids are in balance but sometimes this can change for simple reasons such as an irritating soap or bubble bath or even bacteria from your poo getting in your vulva area (see pages 185-186). Your fluids shouldn't be very smelly, in particular fishy or metallic smelling; strange coloured, for example greenish, grey or very yellow; chunky or lumpy or like cottage cheese; or have a sudden change in volume, for example much more than you are used to. Your vagina and vulva should not be red or itchy or swollen either – these could be signs of infection which can be easily treated. If something isn't right, speak to a grown-up you trust or ask if you can see a doctor.

YOUR FEELINGS

Use this part of the cycle chart to track your feelings each day. By doing this, you can start to notice any patterns throughout your cycle and how you are feeling. This might help you because you might notice you *always* feel a certain way on a certain day of your cycle. You can then decide what to do about this. If it's a difficult feeling, for example you always feel sad around a particular time, you could decide that you will set some time aside on these days to do positive activities that make you feel good. Or if you know you always feel happy and bright on certain days, you can plan activities that need you to have this type of energy.

There won't always be visible patterns to your feelings, and there will always be other influences on your feelings besides your cycle. But even if you don't find lots of cycle connections, checking in with and

recording how you feel each day, and taking action to
love, nurture and look after your emotional health, will
be very helpful for you. Use these four easy-to-draw
emoji faces to record your feelings:

✶ SMILEY FACE

Use this face on the days you feel mainly happy.

✶ SAD FACE

Use this face on the days you feel mainly upset or sad.

✶ MEH FACE

Use this face on the days you feel mainly in
between or a bit 'meh'.

✶ ANGRY FACE

Use this face on the days you feel mainly cross,
annoyed or angry.

If there is another feeling that you want to record,
you can always invent a new emoji for that feeling
or just write the word.

Pssst ... all feelings are normal and human. It's what we do with our feelings that's OK or not OK. For example, if we are angry, and we hit someone, it's not the feeling of anger that's wrong, it's the behaviour when we hit. It's OK to be angry, but it's not OK to hit people. As we grow up, we have to work out ways to control the way we behave and react when we are having difficult feelings. We can also learn safe and healthy ways to express our feelings, for example, if we are angry, we can talk to someone we trust, go for a long walk, write in our diary or shout into our pillow.

YOUR ENERGY LEVELS

Use this part of the chart to record your energy levels each day, using simple arrows. Use an 'up' arrow for days when you feel you have lots of energy, and a 'down' arrow for days when you feel lower in energy. Use a dash (–) for days when you feel in between or aren't sure. Look for patterns between your energy levels at different times in your menstrual cycle. If you see regular patterns, you can start to plan around them where possible. For example, day 12 of your cycle might be perfect for going for a run, but day 2 not so much. Don't let this stop you from joining in with everything and saying yes to all the wonderful opportunities that come your way. But do let it encourage you to be kind to yourself and give yourself a break if you need to.

It's OK to listen to your body's needs and take a break sometimes.

IF YOUR BODY SAYS GO DUVET,
GO DUVET!

★ LISTEN TO YOUR BODY – ★
TRUST YOUR BODY – LOVE YOUR BODY!

You might want to track other details about yourself during your cycle, for example your self-esteem, or a certain aspect of your health (e.g. if you have a long-term medical condition or diagnosis such as asthma or autism, you could record how this affects you during each cycle). You could also record your creativity, sleep patterns, the moon phases or even where you are staying (if your time is divided between different homes). You could try tracking different things each month, just for fun and to be curious. To do this, just print out a second chart, and fill them in side-by-side.

Pssst ... Keep a note of changes, Cycle Detectives! While you are in your first year or two of having your periods, your cycle might still be a bit unpredictable. But once you get a bit older, start tuning in to any differences in your cycle. Some people describe periods and cycles as an 'early warning system' that something isn't right – it could be a clue that you need to take better care of yourself, that you are run down or even unwell. Get to know your usual patterns – your cycle length, the heaviness or lightness of your flow, the colour of your blood, the length of your period, your moods – and if something changes, pay attention!

Cycle Superstars!

→ VENUS OF LAUSELL ←
→ 25,000-year-old Stone Carving ←

OK, yes, I know, the rest of our Cycle Superstars are, well,
actual people, but although this mama is made of stone, she
really is worth knowing about. And who knows, maybe she was
a real person, once – a very VERY long time ago. Her carving,
in the meantime, lay hidden in a cave in France for thousands
and thousands of years until it was unearthed in 1911.

'Venus' is the name archaeologists give to lots of similar
carvings they've found from the
early Stone Age, always of
curvy women with big boobs,
big bottoms and big bellies,
thought to be goddesses or fertility
symbols, sometimes used to represent
pregnancy, growth, rebirth or good

harvests. What makes the Venus of Laussel different is what she is holding: an upturned horn in her right hand marked clearly with thirteen lines or notches, while her left hand rests on her belly, over her womb.

So what's this got to do with periods? Well, 13 could possibly represent the number of periods or the number of moons in a year, or it could be a way of counting the days between ovulation and menstruation. Because of its association with the moon and periods, 13 has long been considered a powerful female number. The Venus of Laussel points to her womb and shows us the number 13 – if she could talk maybe she'd say, 'Periods are my superpower – and I totally ROCK!'. Carving notches on a horn or bone that chart the yearly number of cycles seems to have happened elsewhere in history, for example, the Lebombo bone, which at 38,000 years old is considered to be the world's oldest mathematical object. And this *could* mean women were the first mathematicians, because with TWENTY NINE clearly defined notches, the Lebombo bone just might have been the world's first ever period tracker!

★ WRITING A JOURNAL ★

Do you keep a diary? This might be a notebook in which you jot down just a few key things each day, or a place where you record all kinds of thoughts and feelings, as well as the events of your life. Your pre-teen and teenage years are a wonderful time to start writing a diary if you don't already, and if you do this alongside your cycle charts, this will give you even more information about your personal journey through each month.

There isn't a right or wrong way to write a journal, but the following tips might help you get started.

★   Use a blank notebook or a 'page-a-day' diary for the year.

★   Set aside a time each day when you always write. Many people like to do this when they get into bed each night.

★   Don't worry too much or get put off if you miss a day.

★   You could try using a set pattern for diary entries, e.g. 'Today I did . . . . Today I felt . . . . Tomorrow I hope that . . . .'

Build in special sections, for example, at the bottom of each day you could leave space to record interesting dreams (if you have a lot of dreams, this might develop into a Dream Journal!), or each day write three bullet points, for example:

I am grateful for:
* hugs with my dog
* ice cream with my gran
* being healthy.

OR

My goals for tomorrow are:
* say sorry to my friend
* finish my maths homework
* go trampolining.

OR

My best things about today were:
* swimming
* getting extra screen time
* finding my lost necklace.

CHAPTER SEVEN

Looking After Number One

CHAPTER SEVEN

Looking After Number One

Periods are part of growing up, and growing up means starting to learn to look after yourself more and more. Although it's a new and daunting feeling, it can also be really exciting to begin to feel more independent, and to take charge of looking after you – inside and out! This is sometimes called 'self-care'.

This book is full of 'self-care' ideas, from the Body Buddy Boxes to charting your cycles and learning about and celebrating your first period. This final section will give you a few more ideas on how to look after that VIP – you!

SURFING THE EMOTIONAL WAVES

Let's talk about how to **SURF** the ups and downs of puberty emotions. And like real life surfing, this is

NOT easy to master! Confession: I've never actually *been* surfing, but I know that if I *did* go, I would not be able to stand up on the board **AT ALL**. Except maybe just once, when, after three hours of trying, I would probably manage to stand for a whole **3.4 SECONDS** before falling off, whacking my chin on the head of a handsome instructor called Brad, crying because it really flipping hurt and then, nearly dying from embarrassment, scuttling off up the beach feeling really daft in my wetsuit.

And that's a bit like the emotions of puberty, isn't it? We can talk about 'surfing the waves' if we like, but most of the time, it just feels like they are crashing around us while we flounder about in the ocean. It can sometimes feel like we just *can't* do it, we *can't* manage and we are *never* going to get the hang of it.

It's perfectly normal to feel this way, and a lot of it is due to – you've guessed it,

HORMONES!

As your body goes through some big changes, the hormones you produce can make you feel very up and down, and emotionally, well, all over the place!

But it's unfair to put *all* the blame on hormones. Another reason why you can feel this way is because of the emotional side of growing up. You are probably starting to notice a lot more of the adult world, from stuff that's happening on the news to the lives and relationships of the people around you, and sometimes, you might feel worried or anxious. You are also discovering who **YOU** are, and this journey towards finding your own identity can feel everything from awkward to mind-bogglingly crazy.

In your school life, you might find changes happening in your friendship groups. As you focus more on who you are, you might find you don't have so much in common with some of your friends from earlier in your school life. There might be other falling outs that you just don't understand or can't explain. These situations can cause difficult feelings and upsets as everybody readjusts and tries to get back up on their surf board.

Then, at home, you might find the waves are even *bigger*. One minute you feel fine and the next you are absolutely

FURIOUS!

Then, a bit later, all you want is to cuddle up and watch TV with the people you just yelled at. They, meanwhile, think you should get an 'early night' because you are 'a bit tired and emotional'. This suggestion makes you

FURIOUS again and, *crash*, another big wave hits the beach without you on it.

It's tiring being in the sea. Keep trying, and remember, you will soon be in the beach café wrapped in a fluffy towel and drinking a hot chocolate.

In the meantime, remember: **S.U.R.F!**

✦ S – SLEEP WELL.

Yes, I know, it's annoying to say, but if you get a good night's sleep, everything will seem a bit easier to handle. Sleep helps you to process emotions and events, and enables your brain to better regulate and control your feelings. Fresh sheets, a tidy room, blackout curtains in the summer and no screens for an hour before bed can help. (They give off a blue light that can disrupt your sleep hormones!) Listen to your body when your body needs rest.

✦ U – UNPLUG.

Yup. Screens. I know, they are fun, and a bit addictive, but try to have some downtime each day which *doesn't* involve watching dog videos. Have a bubble bath, write in your diary, read or get some exercise. These are all good alternative ways of treating yourself and relaxing. The online world can also be unhelpful for our mental health, in particular if we spend too much time comparing ourselves to others, which can affect our self-confidence.

✦ R – RELEASE FEELINGS.

Try not to keep all your feelings bottled up inside you. Instead, find someone to talk to, even if it's just to say, 'I don't want to talk today, I'm feeling a bit stressed out.' If you feel comfortable sharing your feelings with a parent, do this – they will probably be very relieved to connect with you and give you a hug if you need it. And if talking isn't what you are in the mood for, write down your feelings (even if you screw them up and put them in the bin), or try drawing, painting or writing stories or poetry – creative art can make you feel much better.

✦ F – FEED WELL.

Just like sleep, you need lots of nutritious food when you are growing fast, and as you might know if you've ever got 'hangry', hunger can affect your feelings, too. Healthy eating doesn't just mean fruit and veg either, it means balance – so as well as your five a day, don't forget carbs such as wholemeal bread, crackers, pasta; and proteins such as meat, fish, cheese, eggs and nuts. Keep hydrated by drinking water regularly. Avoid too many sugary and processed foods, but it's OK to treat yourself to a cake or a biscuit from time to time – when you are learning to surf, you burn a lot of energy!

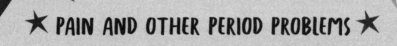

★ PAIN AND OTHER PERIOD PROBLEMS ★

OK, here is the truth: periods can be uncomfortable, inconvenient or even painful, but you've probably already heard that. It's not a big secret. However, here's something that might get talked about less: there's a difference between 'pain' and 'suffering'. While pain might be part and parcel of menstruation for many of us, *suffering* is not, and if you are suffering, it's really important that you speak up. Your period should *not* be so heavy or painful that it affects your ability to go about your day, be in school or enjoy your usual activities.

If your period pain is severe, or if your flow is very heavy or suddenly get heavier than you're used to, it's a good idea to ask to see a doctor, so that they can make sure this is not caused by an underlying health problem. One of these problems is a condition called endometriosis, which is quite common and can cause very heavy and painful periods, so do mention it to your doctor and ask them to do all they can to rule it out.

Sometimes doctors will prescribe the contraceptive pill (sometimes called the Pill) if you have period problems. The Pill was originally designed to stop ovulation as a way to prevent pregnancy in women who wanted to be sexually active but not have babies. However, because it stops you having a natural menstrual cycle, it's sometimes given to younger girls to treat painful, irregular or heavy periods. Some people do find the Pill helpful, but it's important to remember that if your problems are caused by a health problem (for example endometriosis), the Pill is not *curing* that problem, it is only taking away the *symptoms*. Before taking the Pill to help with period problems, it's a good idea to try to work out what's *causing* the symptoms and see if there are any other options that you and your doctor can explore.

It's also a good idea to remember that problems with our periods and cycles can be a sign that we are not looking after ourselves as we should. So check-in with yourself. Are you getting enough sleep? Are you eating enough and is it fresh and balanced? Are you stressed? Are you worried? Are you moving your body enough?

Periods can also be impacted by ill health in other parts of our body. Sometimes a physical or mental health condition can affect our periods, causing them to stop or be painful. This is why it's always really important to look after your physical and mental health with rest, nutritious food, good self-care and plenty of sleep. They might not be able to cure your condition, but they won't make things worse.

As well as pain, there could be other reasons you may have a less than positive experience of periods. It's always good to talk to a trusted adult or your doctor if you are worried or need any more information.

✦ REMEMBER: ✦

- ☑ Periods do not = suffering!
- ☑ If you *are* suffering, talk to an adult you trust and visit a doctor.
- ☑ Period problems can be an early warning sign that you need to take better care of yourself.

★ PERIOD PAIN REMEDIES ★

For mild to moderate period pain try:

★ Hot-water bottle or heat pad: snuggle up in bed or on the sofa and apply heat where it's sore, either on your tummy or lower back.

★ Bath or shower: soaking in the tub or a nice warm shower can help you feel better.

★ Ibuprofen or paracetamol: if you're in a lot of discomfort, speak to your grown-up about taking some paracetamol or ibuprofen (but not aspirin, as you shouldn't take this if you are under 16). Don't be tempted by pain tablets that claim to target period pain – these can cost about 15 times more than a bog-standard packet of ibuprofen which is exactly what they contain – and you thought the Tampon Tax (see page 63) was a rip off!

★ Chocolate: well this one might only help because it cheers us up, but hey, it's worth a try, right?! Dark chocolate is said to be particularly good because it contains magnesium, which can relax muscles and ease cramps. But if you'd rather have a Crunchie, I'm not going to stop you.

★ Movement or exercise: walking, running, swimming or other ways of moving your body can help, especially with mild period pain. Listen to your body on this one, and if it feels like it will help, try it.

★ Chamomile tea: this is a herbal tea made from chamomile flowers. Some people find it relieves period pain, particularly if you drink it in the run up to your period. It's thought that it helps because chamomile tea contains glycine, which relieves muscle tension. As an alternative, add a small amount of grated ginger to hot water – this can also help. You can also add a lemon slice for a delicious taste combo!

If your period pain is so severe that remedies like these don't help at all, do not put up with this, and talk to an adult you trust about seeing a doctor. And of course, make sure you are eating fresh healthy and nutritious foods, drinking water regularly, moving and exercising, resting and relaxing and taking good care of yourself, because all of this can affect your cycles!

Listen to your body – trust your body – Love your body

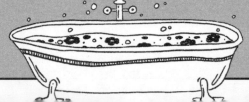

★ KEEPING YOUR BODY CLEAN AND FRESH ★

Oh yikes. Have you seen some of the products in the same aisle as the pads and tampons? Lines of bottles and packets of wash, powder, gels, wipes and more, usually with the word 'intimate' on them somewhere or saying they are for your *'feminine area'*.

Well shock news: none of them are needed. You don't even need **SOAP** to clean your 'feminine area' – and by this we have to assume they mean your vagina and vulva – although for some reason it seems like they're a bit too shy to use the proper words!

★ YOUR VAGINA IS SELF CLEANING!

That's right, your vagina doesn't need any soap, it's designed to clean itself. It does this with the help of its own colony of 'friendly bacteria', and with vaginal fluids to 'wash it out' and keep it balanced and healthy. If you wash your vagina with soap – and even if it's called a fancy name like Fabulously Feminine Intimate

Freshness Gel, it's still **SOAP** – then you risk upsetting the chemical balance in your vagina. This can actually make it unhealthy, even encouraging problems such as itching, redness or infection.

✦ YOUR VULVA ONLY NEEDS WASHING WITH WATER!

You DO need to wash your vulva (that's the bit on the outside, the vagina is the bit on the inside, see page 31). But you only need to wash it with water, either by having a bath or rinsing between your legs in the shower. You don't need to use anything like flannels, sponges or brushes, just your hands. When you have your period, you might like to wash your vulva more often, in particular if you are using period products that are worn externally, such as pads.

✦ YOU ARE NOT SMELLY!

Well actually, that's not quite true – we are **ALL** smelly if we don't wash, whether we are male, female, young, old, having our period, ovulating or otherwise! What I mean is, being a girl, being on your period or being anywhere else in your cycle, doesn't make you smelly. You don't need special 'girl soap'. Your vagina and vulva, when fresh, healthy and clean, smell just like most other people's vagina and vulva. They don't smell like roses or lavender or Fabulously Feminine Intimate Freshness Gel because *they're not supposed to*. They are supposed to smell like vaginas and vulvas.

As you are growing up, you might find you sweat more than you did when you were younger, that you have more vaginal fluid and, of course, you will start to have your period. For all of these reasons, it's a good idea to wash, shower or bathe, and change your clothes, regularly – ideally every day or every other day. This way you won't get pongy! Well – that's one less thing to worry about!

Pssst ... did you know that when you wipe after going to the toilet, you should always try to wipe going from 'front to back'? What this means is that you should always be very careful not to get any poo or bacteria from your anus, on or into your vagina or urethra. As long as you remember to be careful about this, how you actually decide to wipe is up to you. Oh, and don't forget to wash your hands!

DEALING WITH LEAKS

★ LEAK SITUATION #1: BEDSHEETS

If your period comes unexpectedly in the night, or if your pad, tampon or other product 'leaks', then you might wake up to find a little bit of blood on your bedsheets. If this happens, don't worry, it's perfectly normal and it's almost certainly happened to most girls and women who have ever been alive on this planet. You can ask for help from a grown-up of course, but if you want to win some real brownie points, here's how to sort the problem out yourself. Of course, you might already know how to do this – great – but if you don't, here are some of the basics.

☑ Take your sheets off as soon as you can and run the stains through some cold water. Also run your pyjamas, nightie or underwear under the cold water too and then follow the other stain-removal methods coming up on pages 196–199.

✔ You can just take off your bottom sheet if that's where the period blood has marked, but you can also take the opportunity to change your duvet cover and pillow case at the same time, making it all nice and fresh for your next sleep.

✔ If your period has gone through to the mattress, you can try wetting it with a damp flannel, and then blotting out the water with kitchen roll or a dry towel. Make sure you don't make the mattress too wet and air it well afterwards. If you haven't already got one, talk to an adult about getting a mattress protector to go under your sheet to prevent future accidents.

✔ Once you've done your best with the stains, ask an adult to help you put your sheets through the laundry.

✓ Get some clean bedsheets from wherever they are stored in your house. Bottom sheets are not too difficult to put on – most are 'fitted' and just need to be stretched across your mattress so that all four corners are tucked in around the edges. Pillow cases are easy peasy. But duvet covers. Whoahh! Those babies are **TRICKY!** Let me tell you that even grown-ups get into serious difficulties with duvet covers, and often they can't agree on the best way to put the new one on without getting stuck inside it yourself and doing an accidental ghost impression! If this happens, ask an adult to show you their favourite method and then keep practising!

Congratulations if you manage to put on a duvet cover with ease, it is widely agreed to be more difficult than brain surgery and rocket science.

★ DID YOU KNOW? ★
POT PLANTS LIKE PERIOD BLOOD!

Apparently ... rumour has it ... if you are soaking your pads, you can use the water afterwards to water your house plants! Or, if you use a menstrual cup, you can collect your period blood and mix it with about ten times as much water as there is period blood. This is said to work because your period blood contains chemicals known as nitrogen, phosphorus and potassium – all major plant nutrients! You might want to talk to your grown-up before you try this as they probably won't want a menstrual blood spillage all over the new sofa. Be aware that they also might find the idea a bit ... odd or yucky. Explain to them that this is because we have been taught that period blood is ever so slightly gross, but that it isn't any different to the fertilizer containing blood you can buy at any garden centre. If your grown-up still really objects, you can save this idea for when you are a little bit older and have a house, and house plants, of your own.

✶ LEAK SITUATION #2: PUBLIC LEAKS

We all know that periods are something to be proud of, but at the same time, it can feel awkward if you are in a public situation and you 'leak'. So yikes, what **DO** you do when your period arrives when you least expect it or your flow is too heavy for your tampon, and your clothes have a red stain that you feel really self-conscious about? Here's a few top tips for dealing with public period **LEAKS**.

☑ Leaks **HAPPEN**, and they happen to **EVERYONE** who has periods! It's tough if you feel embarrassed in a public place, but try to remember you're definitely not alone. In fact, it might help to visualise your absolute **FAVE** female celebrity having a leak situation – because you can be absolutely sure it's happened to her at some point! Remember – periods are not something to be ashamed of.

☑ Plan **AHEAD**. If you know your period is due, or you are on day one or two of a heavy period, take spare underwear/knickers and leggings with you rolled up in your bag, **AND** wear a pair of period pants or a pad for heavy flow **AND** wear dark clothes, which will make leaks less visible! Double up with a tampon **AND** a pad for heavy days, and check regularly to see if they need changing.

☑ Use the **JUMPER TRICK**. If a leak happens, you might not feel embarrassed at all. However, if you do, you could cover up on the way to the loos by knotting your jumper around your waist so it hangs down over the stain. No jumper? Try holding your bag, jacket, magazine or school books in the right place. If you're wearing a skirt, you can twist the blood-stained patch around to the front so it's easier to cover, or if you're wearing a shirt, you might be able to untuck it and let it hang down to cover the stain.

☑ Get **HELP!** Once you've let a friend or an adult you trust know what has happened, they will be sure to help you out! You could ask them to walk behind you if you have to make a trip down the school

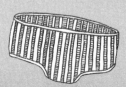

corridors, so people can't see the mark. They might also lend you a pad or a change of clothes, or help you rinse the stain under cold water. Hand dryers in public toilets can dry a patch once you've rinsed it if you don't have any spare clothing.

Keep a sense of
HUMOUR!

It's hard, but one day you will see the funny side of this story and be able to laugh about it. You have joined a club today that every girl and woman gets to join at some point in her life, the PLS (Public Leak Society)!

Cycle Superstars!

LIV STRÖMQUIST
Comic Book Artist

Liv Strömquist was born in Sweden and today she lives in a big city there called Malmö. She started making her own comics when she was just five years old! When she was in her twenties, just like Chella Quint (see pages 17–18), she started making fanzines, and this led to her amazing work getting published in other magazines and comics.

But in 2017, Liv produced some art that many people considered truly shocking. She made a series of images that were displayed on the underground train system in the capital of Sweden, Stockholm, some of which showed menstruating women. One of the images was a black and white picture of a tutu-wearing woman in ice skates, with bright red marks on her leotard where her period had 'leaked'. While some people loved the pictures, lots of other people complained.

One person said they had gone to the subway with their granddaughter and were horrified to have to explain to her why the dancer had blood between her legs. But Liv Strömquist sees this differently: 'To me, that's a great opportunity to explain periods to her granddaughter, to say, "This will happen to you, it's very normal, and this is how the species survives."'

Liv Strömquist isn't the only person who has made art about periods. Other women, like Rupi Kaur (see pages 200-202), use creativity to try to explore what it's like to have periods or start conversations about how people feel about them. American artist Judy Chicago made several works about periods in the 1970s, one of which, a photo of a woman removing her tampon, caused huge shock. More recently, Jen Lewis has made a series of photos of her period blood being tipped through water, called Beauty in Blood, to show that menstruation is not disgusting or shameful.

Period art is called 'Menstrala'. If you made menstrala, what would you make, and what message would you want to give?

TIP

Never wear your best or newest knickers around the time of your period! Save them for other days of the month and get some comfy, cotton 'period pants' that you don't mind decorating with a few accidental leaks. You can also wear your 'period pants' and a pad on the days and nights when you are expecting your period, too – this makes it less likely that you'll be taken by surprise and spoil those new white leggings.

✦ LEAK SITUATION #3: STAINS IN CLOTHES, SHEETS AND PADS

Periods are sometimes a bit cheeky. They don't come on the day you expect them, and then they wait until you've got your absolute favourite pair of underwear on before unleashing your heaviest-ever flow. Or they sneak up on you in the night and spotty-dot your fresh white sheets or your best PJs. And of course, if you decide to use reusable pads, then you will literally deliberately be getting your period blood all over those super-cool designs you spent so long choosing! Whatever happens, it's going to be useful to know how to get blood out of fabric, so here's a few tips:

☑ **Cold Water:** Rinse the garment as soon as you can with COLD water. NEVER use warm or hot water, as this can seal the stain into the fabric and make it even worse! If you are too busy to do anything else, leave in cold water to soak.

☑ **If you have more time:** After rinsing and rubbing the fabric under cold running water, use a standard bar of soap or washing-up liquid and rub this into the stain then rinse. Repeat a few times and see if the stain has gone.

☑ **Still there?** Try a few of these natural stain-removal ideas. (Remember, these will all work best on lighter or white garments. Be careful if you use them on darker fabrics as they might remove some of the colour too.) Ask an adult to help you.

✳ BAKING SODA

Make into a thick paste by mixing a small amount of baking powder with water and rub this onto the stain. Leave for a minimum of 30 minutes or overnight if you have time (but no longer), and then stick your clothing on a normal wash in the machine.

✳ SALT

Plain old kitchen salt rubbed into the stain with a bit of water can help.

✳ LEMON JUICE

Use this alone or mix it with salt or baking soda. Then rub into the stain and leave for five minutes before rinsing.

✳ COLA

Yes, really! Soak the stain in cola for an hour or two, or until you see the stain has gone. Then wash the clothing as usual.

✦ SPIT

Sounds a bit weird, but let's face it, wherever you are
you will always have some of this stuff handy! Your
saliva contains things called enzymes that are good at
breaking down the stain, apparently. And no, there is no
need to **LICK** it! Just put some on a tissue and dab the
stain, or ... spit on it!

If none of the above works, you might like to ask your
grown-up if they can get some stain remover, especially
for blood stains, and help you to follow the instructions.

Body Buddy Box
Getting Compliments

This is a game to play with friends when you all need a
confidence boost. One person at a time is the receiver.
Everyone else takes turns to go round the room and give the
receiver compliments - tell them something that they admire
or that is great about them! The rule is that this is NOT
allowed to be about how they LOOK. Think, 'You are a great
listener' rather than 'You have a nice T-shirt'.

Cycle Superstars!

RUPI KAUR

Poet, Artist, Performer

Rupi Kaur was born in India in 1992 and moved to
Canada when she was four. She writes poems and
illustrates them with simple but beautiful illustrations,
sharing them on Instagram with her 4 million

followers. Her published poetry collections have sold over 8 million copies and been translated into over 42 languages. Impressive!

Rupi Kaur's poems and art are often about what it's like to be human, and how women and girls should have confidence in themselves and their bodies. She frequently shares her message of positivity around being a girl or a woman on her social media accounts. And in 2015, she decided to use photography to explore the taboos around periods.

She uploaded an image of herself in bed, fully clothed, with a small blood stain on the sheets and the back of her pyjamas. She wasn't expecting a particularly big reaction, but the image was taken down by Instagram, who said it went against their guidelines. Rupi Kaur responded by posting the image again, and it was her commentary on the repost that drew the attention of the world, causing the image and story to go viral.

She explained that bleeding every month is a natural process, one that enables the continuation of the human race (whether she chooses to have a child or not). Rupi Kaur's response highlighted that seeing periods as disgusting or unnatural is common, but completely at odds with the beauty and power of them.

Rupi Kaur also pointed out that Instagram had proved her point – responding with the exact same disgust at period blood that her photo was trying to challenge. Instagram later apologised to her and put her image back up, but in the meantime, Rupi had started a whole new conversation about menstrual shame and smashed a few taboos along the way.

★ PERIOD POWER! ★

I hope this book has got you thinking about just how incredible your female body is.

Hopefully you now think that having your period is pretty cool.

You feel a sense of **PRIDE** or **EXCITEMENT** about your period.

Maybe you even

LOVE
YOUR
PERIOD!!!

It's true, there might be times when we feel a bit cheesed off with some of the female stuff we have to deal with – specifically that super heavy, super-crampy period on **THE** day of **THE** coolest ever party.

Then there's the bloating, the headaches, the outbreaks of spots, the stains on our

FAVOURITE UNDERWEAR!!

But hang on a minute! Do we really want to spend most of our lives feeling fed up about something that usually comes around once a month, whether we like it or not?

Instead of feeling negative about our periods, why don't we take time to get to know our body better, understand it more and love what it does. The magic of your menstrual cycle is that it can actually be your friend, giving you different strengths and abilities at different times of each cycle and even letting you know when you need to slow down and take care of yourself!

Your body can do so many wonderful things. Periods and all that go with them, mean that when you're

older, you could even make, birth, and feed a whole new person, WITH YOUR BODY. Making other humans has got to be a superpower, right?!

On the other hand, you might never want to have babies, and that's OK too. We all make different choices about what to do with our bodies and our lives. You are more than just your period – much more!

I wonder what you will do with your wonderful life and what amazing adventures you will have. Maybe you will be a change-maker like some of the Cycle Superstars in this book? Maybe you will travel far and see incredible things? Perhaps you will make a new discovery or invention, or be there just at the right time for someone who really needs you.

Along the way I hope you have beautiful friendships and lots of laughter. You might even find that some of that comes from the solidarity you share with other girls over your menstrual cycle, whether it's giggling in the toilets with a new friend who just helped you out with a tampon or having a movie night with your bestie when you're both on cycle day 1 and in need of the comfort of someone who truly understands.

And, for a big chunk of your incredible lifetime, you'll have another friend alongside you too – your period! It might sound strange, but you may just come to like and respect your period, feeling fond of it as it turns up each month and becomes part of the rhythm of your life.

Having your period is just one part of being a woman, and being a woman is just one part of being human, which is actually pretty fun. I asked my ten-year-old daughter how to end this book, and she said, 'by wishing them Happy Birthday' (she's silly – but silly in a good way). Actually, I hope if you're reading this, you do have happy birthdays, and lots of them, with the best parties, friends who sing to you loudly and extremely big cakes. I hope you have happy periods, from your very first one to your magical menopause, and a lifetime of love and pride in your amazing body with all its clever tricks and eggs, brilliant ideas and other fantastic bits. Most of all,

I hope you always remember to *listen to your body, trust your body, and love your body*, each and every day, as you grow into the person you were born to be, perfect just as you are, yet always changing –

wonderful, brilliant, amazing

YOU.

Resources

USEFUL WEBSITES

Find out more about Period Poverty:
https://periodpoverty.uk/

Write to your school or college and make sure they have free period products available:

http://redboxproject.org/get-involved/periodrevolution/

NHS
https://www.nhs.uk/conditions/periods/starting-periods/

Childline
https://www.childline.org.uk/info-advice/you-your-body/puberty/

You can also call Childline on 0800 1111 or talk to them online at www.childline.org.uk if you are worried about anything (not just to do with puberty) – no problem is too big or too small.

FURTHER READING (For age 9 and up)

The Girls' Guide to Growing Up by Anita Naik

It's Perfectly Normal: changing bodies, growing up, sex and sexual health by Robie H. Harris and Michael Emberley

The Body Image Book for Girls by Charlotte Markey

Step into your power: 23 lessons on how to live your best life by Jamia Wilson

Ruby Luna's Moontime by Tessa Venuti Sanderson
(a novella about starting periods and transitioning to secondary school)

Are You There, God? It's Me, Margaret by Judy Blume

CYCLE CHART TEMPLATE: https://geni.us/MyPeriodCycleChart